Extracting the Warrior

An Anthology of Prison Letters

baz moreno

ISBN 9781448635788

First Printing July 2009

Baz Moreno & Associates, LLC

903B Honey Creek Rd, #296; Conyers, GA 30013-3042

www.bazmoreno.net (404) 300-3945

Printed in the usA by CreateSpace

100 Enterprise Way, Ste A200

Scotts Valley, CA 95066

Acknowledgments

I am appreciative of those who fought to see me survive in a *system designed to emasculate and annihilate melanated beings*. True, others go to prison, but none are affected or have been affected by "the system" as have been Blacks in Amerika because the industry of prison is an extension of slavery.

I am forever apologetic for having introduced such disharmony into the cipher of those whose destiny did not require such a school. I trust that my experience will prevent you from ever gracing the bowels of Amerika.

I am grateful to the individuals who have intentionally or indirectly assisted me in avoiding *'the streets'* and learning to hustle in a different manner since my showing (return home). Your love will not go unrecognized or unappreciated.

Undoubtedly, I thank the people who have nourished me with an organic love, courage, hope, inspiration, ire, comprehension, necessity, talent and strength. I have removed the adornments and embraced my masculinity. As I bathe in blackness – know that this is my armor. With it, I will shield you and improve us.

I would be remiss to not mention Copy Writer, Johanna Crawford. Your attention to detail, concern, firmness and comprehension of grammar, language and context has improved my ability to communicate. One day you will recognize what I intended and desired.

As my pen moves I dedicate the following pages to Owen Malone, Omari Fariyd Dixon, Ishaan Romello Cain, Ferlonzo Hunt, Marquette Malone, Barron Dixon, Aaron Cain, Tralon Bess, Brient Brown, Malaysia Brown, Denise Ternoir, single mothers and anyone who has remained by a loved one enduring isolation and/or incarceration in Amerika's penal system.

And lastly, I appreciate my Elders, but I humbly seek guidance from my Ancestors as the Creative Forces continue to use their collective energies to communicate to me and through me.

Table of Contents

Introduction

I would like to think that my life changed in the latter part of the month of January – the year was 1999. I remember it like yester-day, for this is the time in which I came face-to-face with two unfavorable societal systems referred to as justice and penal.

The younger of my two brothers had previously been to prison in Florida and was, at this time, serving an unjust sentence in the state of Alabama. His survival in prison rested on me. More importantly, his eventual extraction required my presence and attention. Somehow, I had been negligent in receiving the lessons offered by his attraction of misfortune, when I should have been more studious. Besides, the number of cases in which an inmate's constitutional rights weren't violated, in some manner, was minute compared to cases which ignored the state or federal constitution and common sense.

Surprisingly, I overlooked the signs designed to guide me similarly to the way we conditionally accepted a white male walking through the "quarters" in the 70s. The pursuit of a doctorate, fortune, and a life without dilemma had me going in circles. Travels, women, money, family and routine adrenaline withdrawals had fatigued me. I was addicted to the rush - the chase. My thoughts were scattered and my vision was smeared with greed and self preservation.

As I stood in the busiest airport in the world - there was very little chance of me pulling anyone's luggage. I stopped the woman who had willingly bartered my life for her own freedom. I rightfully handed her the luggage that would eventually decide my future. I felt lighter as I picked up my strut, minus her baggage, hope and fears. I had momentarily broken a law by chivalrous standards. Waiting curbside or having my associate catch a cab would have been more appropriate.

"Dr. Moreno," The confident voice belonged to a caucasian wearing a t-shirt and jeans. Holding his authority - a badge. "Can I see your ID, please?"

"You've already identified me." I was indignant as I reluctantly reached for my wallet and prepared to call my attorney. Much of what I did not know that night, I should have learned from the news, newspapers, numerous magazine articles, gossip, movies, history or vanishings. Black men routinely disappeared from our communities for various reasons when I was a child. Most were on a one way trip to jail the day they were introduced to public schooling. As a result of Ancestral denial, depletion of heritage and a growing fascination with materialism our people have forgotten their legacy and become dangerously complacent with the price of being slaves to the anglo mentality and his capitalistic society.

While some of the missing men went to jail, others were splitting their time between two homes. Fathering was increasingly becoming a sport for real men as clueless males turned bedrooms into game rooms. The gap between habits derived from slavery and those practiced today seemed narrow when one considered that a man was defined by how many women he could impregnate and how many kids he could claim. This mentality, however, carried out the notion that merely implanting a seed into a woman was enough to be a man or even worse, a father. This thought process perpetrated itself into the minds of our men and created a contagion of broken homes. Angry women and destitute children were becoming the norm.

A many other men went off to work in other states, while others wished to avoid the responsibility of providing for a family all together and voluntarily ran away. Some men died miserably as a result of violence or disease. And a few more were called to serve in the military. However, the most pronounced disappearances were those of Black men who were dragged off to penitentiaries. Today, most prisoners gladly help build what we now call prisons or work camps. However, as a boy, when they returned to society it didn't matter why they were sentenced because they were all perceived as killers in my eyes. Public schooling had taught me to fear my own people. Eventually, I hated any Black man who didn't act like the white male. It was only natural for me to fear and despise Black men, while respecting anglos. I had practiced fear, love, and respect for all the wrong reasons.

In all actuality, my life should have changed when Omar was inducted into the prison industrial complex, but I hadn't learned the true meaning of 'vicariousness'. Sure, I had used the word vicarious enough to have known that by imagining or meditating on the feelings and actions of my brother that I could've saved myself some discomfort and hundreds of thousands of dollars in legal fees. But, I didn't. Omar wasn't the first person I had seen hauled off to prison and on their way to rehabilitation or what I learned to see as emasculation. I had been desensitized and taught self hatred. I accepted their leave as an excursion without ever thinking that they were in any type of jeopardy. I never contemplated that their temporary leave was jeopardizing the entire community. And for this reason, I believe, I wasn't affected by the absence of any individual who suffered a forfeiture of freedom. I eventually learned that anything probable in Amerika - was possible anywhere in the Afrikan Diaspora.

With the loss of my brother and the impendent loss of my wife's freedom and endangerment I began to view things in a different perspective. These changes in perception affected my relationship with my spouse and improved my status with my brother. After Omar's incarceration I accepted collect calls from prison; mailed articles and books to prison; made contacts in the prison(s); spoke to prison administrators; and facilitated my brother's growth. Whether it meant negotiating with klansmen, presidents of universities or retaining attorneys - I was determined to liberate my brother.

Karma had a way of telling me that I had not escaped lessons which I should have learned. Looking back – I had been pretty damn selfish, indeed. Unfortunately, my troubles began once I materialized as a melanated being. Something about being Black suggests that one has materialized on this plane to gain from lessons in strength and wisdom. If such lessons are mastered, one will attain a beauty, peace, and completeness that is only definable by soul.

As I educated Omar, I had no idea that he was being groomed to give back to me all that I had freely given to him. The majority of the following letters are a selection from correspondence that I received from my brother during the year of 2001. The letters are raw, real, warm, comical, educational, painful, revealing, truthful, unpolished, and at times, embarrassing. It's my hope that others can gain insight and find a hint of themselves in the selected letters written to me by Omar.

Chapter 1- Expectations of Failure

Only a handful of people knew that my parole date had been approved. Instinctively, I knew that I couldn't trust my destiny to the pessimistic attitudes of individuals who had systematically learned to want nothing for themselves.

My ritual morning shower, the last one I would take in captivity, was longer than usual as I tried to leave behind some of the filth that I had accumulated over the numerous years of incarceration. And though, I wanted to eat - I couldn't. Instead, I wanted to purge my body of all the *waste* the system had offered as a meal.

I sat quietly as groups of inmates anticipating the work day filed to the holding area to wait their call to beautify the city and of course, remind the people that crime *doesn't* pay. However, any government utilizing prisoners to minimize tax increases, hiring freezes or population enhancement would disagree because prison labor prevented much of the problems associated with budgets of smaller governments: making most governments – public enemy, number one.

"Moreno, you plan on leavin' or... you scared?" The lieutenant had seen a many male walk through those doors that led to disappointment; both directions. And I had seen the energetic, oppressive, slim negro officer move from sergeant to lieutenant over the four year period in which I slaved as a firefighter and existed as an *enmate* (not inmate). In a nonchalant manner I confirmed that I was ready. He handed me a box and spoke loudly. Several inmates yelled out to claim items that I no longer had because I had prematurely offered my belongings to individuals in need of food, toiletries, stationery and books without detailing my generosity. Granted, these things carried little value in the streets because they were common.

"Who comin' to getcha?" One female guard asked. "I know you ridin' home in style." I said nothing. It didn't matter. I wanted her and those watching to think that I was no different than any other inmate leaving a state of oppression despite how others viewed me. I was taking the bus. There is neither a dignified way of dying nor a more proper way of leaving prison than to just leave. I made no promises. I lost no tears. I saved all my energy as I anticipated the moment that the department of corrections faxed its standard letter of confirmation to grant or postpone my parole approval. I could not live another day *adentro* – in prison. I had done enough pull-ups, push-ups, squats and sit-ups to know that I was ready to test the most talented guard willing to have me remain as the property of his government. I was as mad on the day of my departure as I was on the day of my wrongful conviction. I had returned my oppressor's god along with other things that retarded my growth. The baggage I had thrown back would make my exodus easier.

The boys watching me prepare to exit their "home" were silent. I knew that I was a living testament of strength, wisdom and beauty. I didn't talk about the sex or food which I was thought to desire, for my oppressors composed the head and body of the *belly* that I was departing. I would remain in the same funk. Admitting that there would be no limousine waiting for me outside came with ease. After all, I had worn enough masks to tell a lie without talking.

The contents of the box were no surprise. And I didn't treat the box like a belated Christmas gift. I wondered who I had become. It is hard to be a man when someone else is choosing your clothing. Yet, I donned the oversized khakis, a tight, white button-up shirt and a pair of white K-Swiss sneakers that I had managed to keep clean since the first time I was told that I would parole. The bus ticket, a check from the monies I did not spend and papers instructing me where to report were given to me in an envelope. I walked through the dining area as the inmates marveled. Some wished me well and others wished that they were me. Yet, some swore that I would 'be back soon' as if I were leaving on a pass.

I held tightly to my two net bags filled mostly with books, a few pair of boxers, white socks I had no use for, white t-shirts I wouldn't wear and a little hope. Really, I had *nothing*.

"C'mon, Moreno. You gonna be late for the bus, *mane*." The lieutenant was excited and rushing as always. "Sarge ready to take you to the station." I casually made my way through the last gate, while absorbing all the expectations of my detractors. I climbed into the van. Front seat. No cuffs. I took in all the sights that had entertained me and encapsulated my potential for too many years. I intentionally avoided answering questions as the van moved me closer to an oppression that *inmates* in the free world rarely noticed. I remained observant. I exited the van without exchanging pleasantries with the officer who would return to the prison to assist in suppressing and overworking Black males and pampering disadvantaged white boys. I stood looking and wondering what I would do with the remainder of my life. I reached into the depths of my bag and fished for my cell phone. There! The signal came quickly. The concrete and steel composing the prison had obviously been a problem for my particular service. "I'm here - bus station." I studied the peculiar store doubling as a bus station with floral gifts, second-hand shoes and vintage clothing; a few chairs. It was early morning. Rural life is so much slower than life in the city.

The make-shift bus station hadn't opened and I only hoped that the bus was not so full that I would have to sit with the overweight woman waiting to board the bus - if my call was not received. Looking in both directions and checking my watch, I casually walked towards the convenience store.

"Morning! I'd like to cash this check." I said as I reached to hand it to the Pakistanian woman elevated behind the counter. She looked it over and thoroughly scanned me from head to toe. She fumbled through some papers and gave me a last cursory glance. The kind of look that made one grab their shirt at the armpit and sniff.

"I can't cash your check." She had no sympathy in her smug, accented tone. I asked no questions as I accepted the check accompanied by an envelope. Nubian had arranged to leave three $20 bills, a $50 bill, two $10s and three $5s just days after I confirmed that I would be leaving. As I exited the store, my car pulled up. Squeaky was smiling. My eyes strained for vision as tears dissolved the film preventing me from seeing the dirt which awaited me. Our embrace was strong. Squeaky was the type of enemy that had kept me fighting for my life. In his world - being from California was more important than our common denominator of blackness.

"I told you I was comin', baz. Hard getting' away from my girl. She wanna know everything! She thinkin' I'm with some other broad." His smile was sincere, but he was a bit uneasy with me. "Besides... she pregnant."

"No problem. I spotted the car at the gas station." I smiled and thought how unfortunate I had been over the last eight years to have missed the excitement of a woman. "So – you got a baby on the way? That's a beautiful thing, man." He sensed that my question was rhetorical. I had always emphasized 'family'.

"I got some stuff for you in the trunk. Met your mom and sister last night. She crazy." I automatically knew he was speaking of Chelsea. "Ol' *moms* is nice. They really love you, baz." His sincerity indicated that he was a messenger of some sorts. He was delivering words to an individual who'd won, lost, sat on the bench and was thinking of re-entering the game without as much as a scrimmage. Emotions were absent. Love wouldn't heal my pains without restraining me.

"I need to get out of these clothes, homey." Nothing he said was news to me. And nothing was factual or permanent. It would take time to prime my emotions for a world that had robbed me of my 30s and made being a "*nerd*" so un-cool.

"*Yes, sirrrr!*" Squeaky had picked up a southern coolness to add to his *Cali* madness and C.R.I.P. style. "I got that pair of pants for you. Plus, your sister gave me some of your clothes." Somehow, someone had saved something from my past. Inanimate, valueless objects are the easiest, no doubt; especially, if no one has use for them. And at 5'6" it is unlikely that some corn-fed kid would appreciate my taste in clothing. And wearing cowboy boots was so not cool that three pair were with my belongings.

After changing my clothing, locating the money and cherishing the passport that my sister had hid in my documents, I gathered papers to look over as we journeyed into my future. I positioned myself in the passenger seat. The ride seemed cold and long. Squeaky made no mention of the $11k he owed Alex and me. And out of respect, discipline and pride, I avoided bringing it up. Besides, it had to come up in the next three hours of conversation en route to Atlanta as he complained of the economy. I was tired of redneck *krackkas,* policies, rules, inspections, shotgun houses, trailers, plantations and forever cooperative, seasoned negroes. I was ready to pick up the pace, blend into society and phase out any bullshit in phase with normalcy.

My life had dramatically changed and I would never forget the *kids* I had left behind in prison. Of course, I would not soon forget the many fools I had met, either. For this reason, I know that education, extended family and simply 'looking out' as in an apprenticeship program, in a Kemetic-centered sense, are the keys to saving our warrior scholars who have yet to be identified or tested.

I took in the sights and fought my emotions as I read mail, looked over bank statements, flipped through photos and reminisced. The yellow papers in the bulky manila envelope had gotten my attention. Inside were numerous letters from various persons who'd written me while I was incarcerated of course. Dudes from Soledad, Chino, Tehachapi, Baker, and San Bernardino County had written me over the years. I had letters from Mexicans in Georgia and California. Even Nubian's El Salvadorian pilot kept in touch with me. However, the letters that out-numbered and outweighed all others came from Omar Sa'i, my youngest brother. I had letters from women throughout the Caribbean, Latin America and the united States, but my brother's letters tugged at my heart. His letters were valued like the Afrikan centered letters I had received from Dr. Llaila Afrika, IM Nur, and Mwalimu Baruti. I had an assortment of letters from authors, professors, clergymen, psychologists and laypersons that I had written, questioned or befriended. Had I been on the streets, I would not have bothered to write any of them in the manner that I did.

Certainly, my anglo-plotted abduction had served a purpose. I opened a letter from Omar and began to read. His handwriting was nothing special, but it was neat and legible. Each letter seemed to be identical until I began to read and reminisce. I had taught my youngest brother and with pen and paper he returned the strength, love, courage, encouragement and wisdom.

"Squeaky, if you're tired," I looked up to check the traffic. The car had swerved as he veered to the right and realized that he was off the road. "I can drive. Remember – I have my driver's license." I had driven a fire engine for a fire and rescue unit for the last four years. And I hadn't had to trust anyone's driving for the last eight years and two months, while not handcuffed. Randomly, I fumbled, unfolded and then selected a missive to read, while Squeaky struggled with a slumber that was indicative of the state of my people.

Chapter 1- Expectations of Failure

3/19/00

Dr. Moreno,

It's always a pleasure to hear from you my brother. Your printed words on paper mean more to me than a phone call because you took the time to write, therefore your energy and effort is what made it all sincere. You are my strength and your struggle is my struggle so together we will keep struggling. If our Creator is responsible for all things then I find it wrong for you to regret your misfortunes because the script for your life has already been written and you are a puppet on strings being controlled by a power greater than yourself. So, don't sit around counting mistakes and time but do make your time count by studying your mistakes and the mistakes of others. I used to spend a lot of time writing you to inform you of my transformation but it didn't save you or Makaarim. I realize that all the knowledge in the world is not worth a damn if it is not used properly and at the proper time. My dear brother, I say this on everything I represent and on everything I love... if I have to sacrifice my life or do my time to the door like Nelson Mandela, then I'm willing to do either one or both if it will allow my two loved ones to be free from these prison walls. Forgive me if I sound crazy but I mean every word because this place is not for people such as you two. Here I have a God and a Goddess dipped in the Green Light and every word they speak brings life into existence, which reminds me of the Sun that sits 93 million miles away, so why not call them Suns Of a Deity since they both represent 3 in the path of 9.

Love,

Omar

Squeaky continued fighting the sleep as I searched for another letter. I told my pooped friend that I would drive when he decided to stop for gas. I unfolded another letter. Slightly older. One from earlier in my journey when I was at California Institution for Men in Chino, California. At the time of this letter, I had accepted that I was doing time.

10/10/99

Dr. Moreno,

I send peace with this letter and I hope it find you at ease but still struggling without any weaknesses. I'm still by your side in this struggle but due to the distance between us my assistance is limited. I find myself missing you a great deal. Sometimes we admit that we are independent but in actuality we all depend on each other for existence because as soon as someone such as a guide depart from your life, your co-dependency kicks in. In other words, I haven't been the same without you. Bro, I have a different view on life due to new acquired information but for now I have nowhere in here to focus my energy because no one comprehends, and at times I get frustrated and feel that I'm wasting my time digesting information that could cost me my life. We people as a whole are not equal and will never be equal because we are of different species of mankind. Some of us come from 9 ether (all existing gases), some of us come from the water, some of us come from the mud, and some of us come from beastiality, therefore we will never find peace amongst each other all because of the human anatomy differences which brings different comprehension levels. I hate to throw you off track with my letter but I was writing to let you know that I'm still striving. I received your letter from Chelsea and I'm glad to know you're doing better. Continue your studies and concentrate not on just getting out but staying out. Remember my political prisoner friend (Sekou)? Well, I help him on week-

ends in the law library as a clerk so I'm obtaining information dealing with law. I'll write again soon. I love you.

Your brother, Omar, in the struggle...

"You alright, baz?" Squeaky remembered enough about me to detect that I was holding back. I couldn't talk. It took every muscle to keep from crying. I smiled at the idea of Omar misspelling *bestiality*. It is what it is!

I wasn't sure why I had forwarded these letters to Alex for safekeeping, but they were back in my possession for some reason.

"I'm straight. You can pull over at any time and I will drive, bruh." I knew that reading the letters was going to be laborious and taxing - when I was quite uncertain about my emotions. I put the letters away as we exited.

Chapter 2- Falling for Nothing

Warrants from the governors of California and Georgia had authorized my extradition to Georgia. I was prepared to argue that I was not the *straw man* in question. In addition, I never wrote my name using all capital letters. However, by retaining an attorney I had unknowingly waived my rights. Regardless, I was now in Georgia and it was nothing like California. The nine months of southern living hadn't been hospitable. And the decreased volume of violence hadn't quite allowed me to adjust to the docile, fearful, be-a-good-boy style.

Had I served time in Georgia before serving time in California, I would have been raped or killed. Period! The California Department of Corrections housed some of Amerika's toughest thug homos and sissies. Amongst the boys were revolutionaries, political prisoners, scapegoats, visionaries and men that once made snatching anyone of color something to think about. Every day was tense. And yet, I was anxious about the "Chain Gang" and other's interpretation of the flawed system. Something about slavery scared me. But I was excited about completing my degree because I was told that by doing so I could reduce my time. My attorney arranged for me to be shipped to a prison that encouraged education. What I got was a camp of confused, sexually active boys with a passion for men or what they called *trade*.

My period to earn my degree would be abbreviated by racist programming, intolerance, impatience and my struggle to strengthen the *warrior* within. And my initiation to the stench of Georgia's belly would be swift, funky and frightening. It smelled no different than that of California, but it consisted of far more parasite agents. Such agent provocateurs soiled an already dirty system and assisted in identifying and diagnosing the existence of Amerika's funk.

I am not sure what brought about my anger - other than me being in prison. But, my attitude had changed considerably. I was fighting my personal demons, the demons of the system and every individual who refused to stand up to the system. My frustration was accompanied by the argument that a revolutionary Afrikan would not and could not be a homosexual. Little did I know because intelligent, strong, hard-on-the-outside-soft-on-the-inside dudes with black skin were making noise.

January 2001

Dr. Moreno,

Glory to be Anu as the ink required to write out these words. I am anxious, not to return to devilishment, but to assist Gravity with the legal process that will deliver Che and Black Rose from oppression. I am ready to help my loved ones and willing to sacrifice in order to bring on a change. My life doesn't begin until Che's and Black Rose's current living conditions end. Failure, fear, pressure, and hate are not the fuel that drives me. What drives me is the fact of having something to live for and that something is what will keep me focused. Poverty isn't for 3L9 and never will be again because it was poverty that caused the real face of oppression and racism to appear to me. I am not a Captain-Save -A -Hoe or super nigga so those that are entering, embracing, and accepting poverty will remain in poverty if it is left up to me to assist them. You and I and others that know the TRUTH are our people's messiahs and we must teach and save only those of our BLOODLINE that wants to be saved. You see, every prophet in the Holy Scriptures were sent to their own people to save their own kind. Keep that in mind and think before you reach towards a negro that didn't agree with the science you were trying to kick in his ear. You can't go around trying to beat the truth in a negro or even waste your time arguing about information that another human being wrote down. If I look up to you as a mentor, then you are telling me that it's okay to beat the truth in someone that disagrees with me? We are about peace my brother until and only until they try to destroy S.O.D. as a whole. You have children of your own that you must teach so don't waste your time on deaf ears and closed minds. Much love to you Dr. Moreno and I need you at home. I love you always....

-Omar-

I was rather popular at D. Ray James - a privately owned prison. Word traveled fast that I was there. I had a tattoo on my right forearm with some funny writing (Nubic) and a six-pointed star (Star of David/Shield of Abraham). It was rumored that I was knowledgeable about Islam. Of course, "penitentiary Muslims" were known to be more disciplined, intelligent and stronger than other inmates. I had no desire to unite with anyone's movement. Neither the Five Percent, Sunnis, Nation of Islam, Moorish Science, Yahweh Nation, brothas claiming allegiance to the Nuwaubian Nation nor any other sect had to concern themselves with me. I wasn't interested in being an *amir* or an *imam*. I already had a title that I didn't want or need; an earned felon – they called me.

Nonetheless, I satisfied my displeasure with religion by assisting a brotha from Atlanta with a strong interest in bettering the conditions of Islam in prison. After all, this is Amerika – land of opportunity. Amerika caters to Christianity. Christians are everywhere. So, I refused to become a part of the confusion caused by homosexual activity, religious dogma, drugs, and tired women in an environment designed specifically for crippling boys, stagnating men and pacifying the community.

The D. Ray James prison was rightfully considered a camp for the mentally ill. There were roughly 1500 inmates and two thirds of them were gay, bi-sexual or on the *down-low.* A significant number had complications with their immune system. I was surprised at the soft approach of living that most embraced. I turned to my studies and made the mistake of looking forward to the day I would get out instead of using every moment of every day until I left.

January 2001

Dr. Moreno,

Glory be to Anu as the ink required to write out these words. I send peace and love to you my dear bother along with strength to help you overcome your stress. Receiving your letters for his new year gave me hope. As I read between the lines of your scribes I see pain and I feel your struggle. I appreciate your high hopes of me but nothing in life within amerikkkan slave kkkolonies is certain but change and death, so we must keep in mind the reality side. If it's meant to be then it will definitely happen but please keep in mind that disappointment is not a stranger to me. You brought a smile to my face when you said that you would put me against the best. I thank you for the compliment and your confidence in me. I don't want to go against the best but sit, eat and weak amongst those considered to be the best. I want to be like a chameleon and transform at will. I want to be able to walk in any house and fit right in without being detected as a fraud. I like and admire people like Yahweh Ben Yahweh, Carlos the Jackal, and Malachi Z. York because their rhetoric and many disguises are what cause them to survive in a "dog eats dog world". My hat goes off to them because they are smooth with what they do when it comes to controlling people that can't think for themselves. You must learn from the gangstas, pimps, jail house lawyers, con-men, root doctors, and scholars in there because everyone has game that will one day be useful to you. Don't put yourself in a teacher's position, you will know who to teach and what to teach them. There's an old Chinese saying that says "every student will find his teacher" and from my experiences it's a true statement. Remain silent sometimes and let them negroes talk nonsense. Keep in mind that some of the material you sent me was to defend myself and expose my opponent! I used to be quiet until they would step to me for debates and discussions. Words of wisdom that you shared with me I must now share some with you because my overstanding of your confrontations is familiar ground for me. Stand firm in your teachings and everything you live for and love but don't lose focus of your new goals that must be achieved. S.O.D. needs you and M.Y.R.A. needs your expertise, finesse, and business skills. Study hard and earn your Ph.D. because you have to potential to make some noise when you touch down. As far as them punk niggas and homosexuals let them live out their fantasies because they weren't man enough to tell their women that, "hey baby I'm a bisexual and I wouldn't mind if you fuck me in my ass with that vibrator or dildo you got in the closet." Everytime I turn around I got a ex-sissy in my face that has converted to Islam. I guess it's the prostrating that interests them, if you know what I mean? El-Jabur is the ninth attribute of Anu but it's the number nine that I deal with, so please don't think I'm conceited by taking on the name "The Magnificent". I'm keeping OMAR, out of respect for my parents but please send me a few names with meanings so that I can choose one. They can be Muslim, Swahili, Spanish, or etc. as long as they have meaning... Peace and love to Black Rose and Che and I pray for their deliverance. When I meditate those two people are the ones I try to bring into existence. Stay strong and stay beautiful Dr. Mo' because I need you and we need you. 3L9-S.O.D got love for you.

Shalomluk/Wadu,
Omar

My father had made it clear to me that he would be busy and that I was not to call or write. The guy who had taught me to grow and harvest marijuana had turned his back on me. He was disappointed in my survival and embarrassed by my location. He stayed busy for five years. Alex kept money on my books (account) and Omar continued pouring wisdom into my glass... some of the same wisdom that I had banked with him. Ironically, I couldn't stop teaching Omar and inmates took to me like water in the desert.

January 2001

Dr. Moreno,

There are two highlights in my life at this moment that make my days, week, and months go by and if I could capture them like a moment in time, these two highlights would be me receiving your letters and me picking up a pen to scribe to you. I thank you for mentioning my thoughts of organizing but I stopped working on my project because I was too busy putting all of my thoughts, opinions, and feelings on paper and not realizing that if it was to be a project for us then we must contribute to the project. So, I am patient enough to collaborate when I converse with my brothers in order to have an effective system. Speaking of Che, I know he would be popular amongst people that need him the most, but I fear for his well being because of hidden enemies. Che must become familiar with the word infiltration because it is that word that caused the fall of great men and great nations. I appreciate the analysis of "GOD" and the scriptures as well. I'm proud of you for doing your research and for blessing me with more degrees. I'm familiar with what you are kicking and I'm always anxious to learn from my mentor. Speaking of Masons and the letter "G". Yes, that's true about the letter "G" standing for God, Grand Architect, and Geometrist, but only in the lower degrees. As you climb your way up to the top of the Mason-

ic Lodge and its ladder the real meaning of the letter "G" stands for "Gnosticism". According to Webster's New World Dictionary Second College Edition the word Gnosticism is a system of belief combining ideas derived from Greek philosophy, Oriental mysticism, and ultimately, Christianity, and stressing salvation through gnosis. When you reach the top of the Masonic ladder in degrees you will find in their esoteric teachings that the compass and the square are really a male and female copulating and the letter "G" is referring to " G-spot", I'm serious my brother eventhough it sounds absurd. You see, masonry's foundation is based on sex and the reproduction organs. Next time you look at the compass and the square you will see her legs in the air and him on top of her. The Worshipful Master will exchange his "G" for the "All Seeing Eye" when he pass master status. I'm not trying to confuse my few months of studying with your years of studying to build our foundation. I feel good knowing that I can relate to you but also contribute to you. Keep on blessing me my brother with right knowledge and I will do my best to take it with me wherever I go. I'm not too good at explaining or expressing myself on paper to someone I look up to as a mentor but I hope you get something useful out of each of my scribes. I'm still growing, striving, and maintaining but happiness is far from me. I love you always and I hope you are staying strong. I try to stay in touch with Che and Black Rose because that's where I draw strength from. Peace and love to Gravity, my down ass nigga. Dr. Moreno, I got much respect for you and much love for you. Shalomluk wa Wadu.

Sincerely Yours,

Omar

Our letters had to be sent to Chelsea, Daniela or Alex. They would address and mail the envelopes to the appropriate person. The letters had to be written in third person because neither of us could communicate with inmates in other states. I didn't dare tell anyone that my *complement* and brother were doing time. Besides, they were on my visitation list. Therefore, Bruski, B9, and Sa'i were used for *Omar*; Black Rose was an identifier for Makaarim; Ihsaan was Alex; and they affectionately called me *Che*.

None of the names were code names in actuality because we knew each other by such attributes prior to being separated.

Chapter 3- Ugliness of Truth

Despite how tough one is, prison will get the best of any-one. One could easily hallucinate about fun, love, women, money, material possessions and family. Few ever described their challenges or enemies. Enemies were difficult to define, but it was obvious that a many inmates were re-lieved to be without the responsibility of sharing emotions or providing for a loved one.

I was misunderstood by my family. Regardless, I loved them... in a strange way. Juggling emotions as an Nubian in Amerika was underrated. My environment had damaged me and yet, I continued loving even if it meant pretending and tolerating.

February 6, 2001

Dr.Moreno,

Shalomluk, akhutee! I went to visit our homeboy Ski two weeks ago and he seemed frustrated. He says that the facility has been tampering with his legal mail coming in and going out. Every time he writes in legalese or files a petition pertaining to his freedom it doesn't go out. Anything going to the Montgomery area or to the courts the facility will intercept the material and answer it themselves with smart remarks. He says for months now he has been wanting to tell me but didn't want to upset me. I know if you were around he could depend on you to handle all his legal matters. I be wanting to help him but I know nothing about the system or how to deal with these amerikkkans on their level. You see my brother because of situations like this I can't stay focused on my studies. Why isn't Anu, Allah, or Eloh providing me with the knowledge to help Ski, Che, or

Black Rose? Why do we have to continue to suffer in life and for how long? It seems that when I'm passive I can't get shit done but as soon as I become aggressive everything works to my advantage. It seems that being affiliated with certain parties, societies, and people is what causes the judicial system to degrade, despise, and defame an individual. My intentions are good and my purpose for living is even better but second chances in life is the issue. I realize that in order to get somewhere we must go through something but sometimes I feel like King Solomon, hating the fact that my thoughts would be different if I didn't know about certain things. I guess in some situations its best not to know certain things or experience them. Exposure isn't always good! I don't mean to bore you or lead you astray from my letter but my pen won't allow me to stop. I hope you are well my brother and maintaining your sanity. I spend a lot of time thinking of you and I often ask myself, "What would Dr. Moreno do if this was him?" In certain situations I encounter, I wonder how would you handle them? When asked certain questions, I wonder how would you answer them. I spend a lot of time wanting to be like you and live up to your expectations of me. I spend a lot of time trying and wanting to impress my family members. I'm still battling with my gangster mentality but at the same time I try to make all my family members see my new mentality, my new attitude towards life, and my transformation from being immature to maturity. Please forgive me but I must confess that I actually used to lie to people by showing them pictures of your children telling others that they were my own. For three years I used to brag and show pictures of my niece at her dance school saying that she was my daughter. For three years I used to brag about my nephew being in martial arts saying that I was proud of my son. For three years I used to show a copy of my so called daughter's birth certificate born in Escambia County at Baptist Hospital on February 9, 1993, just to fit in with the older guys that looked up to me. I was so hurt for not having a little girl that it disturbed me mentally. For four years I've been hurt by letters from a woman who blames me for losing our son to adoption. For eleven years the loss of my son has been haunting me and it caused me to not give a damn at times. Because of such disturbance I lost respect for women by beating them, misusing them and being unfaithful to them. I'm not making excuses I just want you to feel me and help me deal with these issues for the rest of my life. The fatal blow came when I found out my daughter wasn't mine and then the mother of that child destroyed my life and my family members. I took risks day and night to provide the best for my so-called daughter because I failed as a father to my first son, and then when I found out the truth I started abusing my so-called daughter mentally, spiritually, and mostly physically. Forgive me for my actions, my thoughts, my stupidity, and the pain and suffering that I caused you and your family. This letter to you is the realist shit I ever wrote. I just want you to know that I quit my senior year in high school to prepare for my first son but still failed as a man according to my plans. I'm not writing for your sympathy, I'm writing to keep it real with you my brother. I'm hurting because I feel robbed of my adolescent years and I have hatred for sorry bitches because they prey on the weak and them same bitches come up off of the weak one's ignorance. My life of the streets, correctional facilities, domestic violence, child abuse, drug dealing, and introduction to schools of thought, I am willing to one day put in a book but my naming goal was to turn to my brother for guidance, counseling, and strength. I hope all this doesn't put our relationship in jeopardy. I got love for you and I'm still down with the struggle. This was just an opportunity for me to get this out of my system so I could move on to a better life. I love you and I'm here for you as well.

Shalomluk,

-Omar-

In California I learned to listen to the souls of men. People talked all the time, but what I heard was different than what they were saying. The people interested in my survival taught me to observe and analyze. Omar's letters were his opportunity to release what he, like most prisoners, had learned to conceal. In prison, masks were the best method of survival. Some looked smart, scared, tough, mad, masculine, rich, harmless, and monogamous. Sadly, most were poor little boys frozen in the moment that they were traumatized by their father.

Feburary 2001

Dr.Moreno,

As usual, the struggle continues and I have accepted the fact that pain is normal and happiness is more of an incentive that's very rare. It's hard to surround yourself with a force of peace but I do send you peace and love with every missive. I see that you are still searching for our real father that has no love for us. You are right and exact on your accusations of him and his actions towards us. If all four of us can't love him on one accord then that individual father and son deal won't work. I don't hate that house nigger with his "Willie Lynch" syndrome, it's just that when I see him again I want to have my house in order so he can see that his youngest son finally made something of his life. You see, I've been falsely accused of sexually abusing my own blood and that's a hard pill to swallow coming from family and no one ever offered to help me cope with the situation. All everyone wanted to know, was is it true? It's cool though because there's no possible way for me to stoop that low just to catch a flight from F.W.B to L.A.X to molest my flesh and blood. Put that dude behind you and move forward. If you are looking for that love that you didn't receive as a child then I extend my hand to uplift you and give you that brotherly love that's stronger than our father's just be that perfect father to your children and be that loving uncle to your nieces and nephews. B.J. fears me because I always go against the grain and I don't deal with the mainstream. He will remain a "blue-collared citizen" for the rest of his life because he's afraid to explore and he's a coward. His love for white women replaces his hatred for his black skin and insecurities. I respect his choices in life, as far as his dealings with white people because a house nigger is taught to do certain things. You must remember that his home training and upbringing plays a major role. You see, it was my first felony that woke me up. Remember my case with that white girl? Leave B.J. alone and let him live his life because the more you show him that you need him the more he will disappoint you. It's a game of revenge for him and his game requires more than one player, so don't play it! One day all of us will catch a flight with all our children, wives, and husbands and show up at his doorstep and let him see what he has been missing all these years. That would be beautiful for us all to do that. It would crush him but he would go to his grave knowing that we cared and we tried to love him. Bro, my plans are to leave the south for awhile and Dallas sounds good to me. I need to relocate but decisions are out of reach for me at this moment. I appreciate your previous letter stating that I would make a good husband, but my intentions were to inform you that I was tired of no good low life bitches and hoes. I'm ready and willing to travel to Latin America and the Islands and meet beautiful women of color that respect and worship my dark skin. I want nothing but the best and when I do marry she will be something that I want and need in my life, not something that I have to settle for because I can't do better. Since happiness is such a rare occasion then I must grasp it and hold on to it. Peace and love to them 3L9 guerillas. Suns of a Deity are stacking only dollars... if Atlanta is the black mecca, then let's do it but if Dallas is more promising then let's do it!!!

Shalomluk/Wadu,

Omar

If I was in denial about anything or anyone, Omar had a way of clarifying things that I clearly romanticized about. His experiences and talents permitted him to share uncut, embittered sentiments without me becoming too emotional. Well, my emotions were fast asleep. With each day I was developing dysfunctions and my ability to freely emote was eroding.

February 20

Dr. Moreno,

I send peace to you my dear brother and along with this piece of paper I must set the record straight because I feel like you have misread and misinterpreted my previous letter when I mentioned that I was dealing with self. It seems that when I spoke of my character defects, my mistakes in life, and my search of inner being, you took it as a sign of weakness. I thought that maybe if I became sentimental on at least one letter you would feel and see that other side of me. I believe in balance even after all trials and errors in life. I was always writing about my debates, my accomplishments, and everything positive in my life, but as soon as I started writing about negative forces in my past that steered my thinking and actions you automatically discerned that I was degrading myself. Dr. Moreno, I'm standing on five spinning off six, and slowly striving towards seven which is perfect man. I'm that burning bush that spoke to Moses, with my dark skin, bushy hair, and redness of my eyes that look like flames of fire. I'm the capstone to the great pyramid in Giza and without me it would be incomplete. I stand firm and for me to speak in such a manner there is no way possible that I would degrade, defame, or demoralize myself but I will defend, define, and defy myself, the truth, and those that challenge my family. You are my big brother and I'm your biggest fan and I got much love for you, the struggle, and S.O.D. I do too much around here to uplift the dead man walking and I assist those that need guidance, so please don't think that I have given up. A kkkracker can't break me, make me, shape me, or take me to a level without me willing to go. Amerikkkan slave kkkolonies are for slaves and I'm not a slave but by me being here in amerikkka I was born into captivity involuntarily. I strive for your trust and I work hard for your respect and I will be loyal to you and our family. Let's leave the past in the past because we are not getting any younger. Yes, I'm rebellious because I was made that way and not even you can argue with the laws of nature.

You always speak the truth and your words of wisdom are helpful. While in exile I learned that love without knowledge is nothing. Real love is the strength to make the person you love unhappy if you know it means that it is for the good or the betterment of the person. The kind of love that does "anything" to please the person is the weakest so-called love that you can find. You cannot love me if you fear to tell what is wrong with me and love me if you want to keep a happy relationship with me while seeing me destroy my life. I thank you for loving me and keeping me in check. To take on a new name is to renounce the emptiness and failure of the past and embrace the promise of the future, and I appreciate the names and meanings. I have chosen one and I will represent like the name Omar, for a lifetime! It's true that I have come too far to quit and I never planned on quitting. I won't let S.O.D. down nor will I allow Che and Black Rose to struggle alone. I thank you for the addresses for legal services and in the near future I will use them if necessary but for now I'm not in need because Alex has assisted me by using the phone. I will spread the word about Anthony and Don. I also have new methods for arriving at the post office with my material and I hope your legal matters are handled with care. Liberation for us all will come soon.

Shalomluk/Wadu,

-Sa'i Omar-

Omar had put a number of years, in prison, behind him. I noticed his changes. He seemed to beat me with his strength in every letter. I had no idea of how I would deal with the years ahead. I had been spoiled, privileged, reckless, ungrateful and ignorant in spite of being privy to an education and opportunity. Of course, my good outweighed my bad, but my bad attracted attention - after improper magnification. Day after day, I analyzed incidents from my life. Even if I didn't think I was changing, I was not the same man arrested in the Hartsfield-Jackson Airport. In the future, things would be different.

Chapter 4- Making Sense of Madness

I attempted to hack away the inessentials as I organized my thoughts. I needed to shed pounds the way friends and family had removed me from their thoughts and hearts.

Omar was busy structuring our future, but he had no idea that the pressures he and I were enduring would make us diamonds amongst people who would never dismiss notions of the oppressor despite how rough things were. More embarrassing was the notion that the people who'd fight us the hardest were the people we loved; people who had sacrificed funds for us; and people who begged us to accept the ways and god of our oppressor. Life behind the wall may have limited my access to information and amenities, but it gave me time to dissect anyone opposing my freedom.

March 2001

Dr. Moreno,

I hope all is well and that you are handling your legal matters. Once again thank you for the addresses for the legal assistance but I'm no longer in need at the moment. I know my way around a law library and I was taught pretty well by brothers that I encountered that are political prisoners according to their opinions and beliefs. I try not to put a financial strain on Alex because he has a family to take care of and his assistance to Che and Black Rose is more important to me. I don't ask for much and I don't pick up a phone unless necessary because I think of Che and Black Rose. I'm not selfish and if you think I am then the word 'altruism' wouldn't describe me. Family is important and I thank you for the drawing you sent but why should I study it daily when everything I stand on represents this same picture that's on my right forearm? I studied your questions but I am confused about the application part for our company. I don't think it would be necessary until the three heads converse to form the Deity. Our blood, sweat, and tears will bring our company into existence and then the rest will fall into place. I've been working on this idea of mine since '97 and I would like to make some helpful suggestions for example- (Outline)

Preface

I. Articles

A. S.O.D. Make Laws and Govern

B. 3L9 Execute Laws/Protect Laws And Members

C. M.Y.R.A. Educate/Contributions

D. M. B Entertainment

II. S.O.D.

A. Spirituality

B. Prayers/Rituals

C. Signs/Symbols

III. 3L9

A. Fitness Program

B. Strategies

C. Codes

IV. M.Y.R.A

A. M.Y.R.A Program

B. Contests/ Talent Shows

C. Donations at Charity Events

V. Moreno Brown Entertainment

A. Promoting Events

B. producing/ Managing Groups

C. Performing

VI. Amendments 1-9

I hate to put such an outline on paper but I just wanted to let you know that I don't play or waste time. I got the potential and capabilities to do great things but with my brothers together I know we can accomplish bigger and better things. Don't count me out my brother because my research and dedication is of great value and if I can't invest my time and energy into my dream child S.O.D. then I must move on. We all have plans and we all will succeed individually but unity will be and must be out driving force. I'm not against you, I'm down with you. Please review and feel what I'm getting at. Much love...

Shalomluk/ Wadu,

Omar

Omar's plans gave me something to desire, but my life would be exacerbated by depression, imposed financial struggle, over-qualification, disqualification and inconsideration due to my social status as a felon. I wouldn't need to exaggerate that blackness would further compound my predicament because my willingness to cooperate was based on the fact that the system didn't forecast the difficulties I'd encounter.

In the coming years, Baba Baruti would explain in *Homosexuality and the Effeminization of Afrikan Males* the importance of dismissing the use of the word *mentor*. It only took one explanation for me to discontinue its use and say `jegna`. After all, Mentor had been trusted by Odysseus in *The Odyssey* to raise his son Telemachus. And as a Greek with homosexual tendencies it is clear that Mentor had his way with Telemachus, while Odysseus sought adventure, elsewhere.

March 01

Dr. Moreno,

I hope all is well in your life and that the All is providing you with strength. I appreciate your positive energy and motivational letters they mean a lot to me. Soon we must stop talking and start doing. I'm surprised that you asked me have I been staying in touch with black rose, and I'm sort of surprised that she never mentions it. Che and Black Rose are thought of by me damn near every time I make major decisions or work on a program that could be beneficial to us all. This song is dedicated to Black Rose, which was written by Bruski 7/99.

Black Rose

*Verse One: Born in this western hemisphere with a eastern heart * Gives me reason to touch but her thorns are too sharp * Attempts of pulling her up replanting in soil that's fertile * Sounds good cause I don't want nobody to hurt her * Living on the northern continent Americanized * Fertilizing my flower with a sacred formula that's purified * Instead of recognizing me as a savior she has assumptions * But I'm symbolic of the Messiah saving this black woman * Trying to bring her in the knowledge of self to know who she is * Here in New Babylon ain't where and how she should live * If I start talking 'bout Jerusalem I'll be losing her * She got eyes set on Mecca but somebody been fooling her * I uplift darkness and shift light dig this duality * Religion in her right hand but mines hold spirituality*

*Chorus: From the bush to the bud down to the petals * Straight from the hood through the mud my eyes ain't never * Seen something so rare I do declare my Black Rose * When you blossom with strength your beauty is exposed * Nothing compares to your style and it shows * Imma shed light on Black Rose so she can grow*

*Verse Two: from triple stages of darkness she evolves with colorful meaning * So black can't represent death if her light is still beaming * She's the foundation of civilization with such significance * All eight directions she take brings life into existence * But for some reason she's not ashamed of her slave name * So east bound I'm taking her by way of the astral plane * Make her travel through the school of thought 'til graduation * Help her get in tuned with her inner self through meditation * Cause here in this geo-graphical region there's lots of havoc * But I know where she goes she grows cause she's Asiatic * Imma bind her up while I'm teaching with divine ties * So when she blossoms she'll be reaching towards the Orion skies * And when my waves of rays hit Black Rose on the surface * Her manife-station on this earth will have served its purpose*

Chorus

*Verse Three: Within the nine months that life, mind and motion was being formed * On the physical plane universal truth was being born * In the beginning time never was when Black Rose was not * So Imma help her overstand the mathematics that she got * She's a representative of nine the law of fulfillment * But she needs 720 degrees for some real strength * Her adaptation to living conditions of this environment * Got her acting wild with a ebonic ghetto style accent * Been in this location too long she has adopted their customs * Since they corrupted her sublime mind it's hard to trust 'em * So Imma plug her ears with real facts from the real lies * And run them devils back up the Caucus Mountains through the hillside * Cause I'm her protection revealing revelations as they come * I'm reclaiming my birthright as the Black Widow's Son*

Repeat Chorus (2x)

Everything that Che and Black Rose ever sent me, I studied it through the years and I placed esoteric teachings in a rap song. As you can see, songwriting is a talent of mine. More like a gift from The All. I hope you like "Black Rose" and feel where I'm coming from. I got much love for my brother and I hope and pray that one day you will accept me as I am, with my slang, my gangsta mentality, my cuss words, and my country self. I work hard on controlling my tongue by using correct grammar and using my intellect to make effective decisions. Before I embarrass you I would remain silent, so please remember that. Your decisions on becoming an Imaam isn't a wise decision. You must not involve yourself with such a position nor organization. The system holds that against muslim leaders because they consider them to be too radical and all prison riots are usually incited by an Imaam, so they say. Save energy for M.Y.R.A. and reach out to the Nubian Youth that need to grow. You need to sit down and calm down if you plan on touching down soon. I take heed to your advice but it's my turn to give it to you! Stay strong and remember I love you.

Shalomluk/Wadu, your brother… Omar

I didn't mind learning from Omar or any other *brotha*, but I was not accepting any negro ideologies. Knowledge had always appealed to me. Although, I no longer agreed that knowledge was power. Funny – knowledge was supposed to be power, but the majority was seeking an education. I was educated. Prison helped me to understand knowledge. Some found knowledge and felt incomplete without an education or degree to prove it. What bothered me was the fact that education and knowledge were used interchangeably and those in quest of an education were merely interested in improving their status as chocolate-dipped anglos.

March 2001

Dr. Moreno

Peace unto you my brother, who is the god of the earth and my mentor. All is well my way and nothing has changed. The same struggle with the same unconscious negroes. I'm not mad though because I know eternal pain and suffering isn't my destiny nor my family's. I continue to stay in shape physically and mentally. I exercise enough to make my years in exile look beneficial. I don't focus on strength when lifting light iron because consistency is what brings all results in all activities. Paul paid me a visit but I can't answer your question about what made him do so. The force behind someone's motives are unexplainable at times. Some people want to see how I look and if I'm insane right about now. Some people write me to see if I respond and to see if time is getting the best of me. I laugh because I have proved them all wrong by maintaining my sanity and by standing on the square to represent my family. Paul and I have been cool for years and his intentions are good. I got love for those that got much love for me. I still study but I have laid off from religious material for two weeks now. I get tired of theories and philosophies

because another man's opinions, new points on life, fantasies of gods, and research of human behavior are useless to
me. I deal with those issues but I still wonder how will I
benefit from them? I can sit around with the so-called
scholars of the world and have a decent conversation by
discussing such issues. But still does it have to do with the
upliftment of man? A doctor can't tell me what's wrong with
me until I tell him any symptoms. A psychiatrist can't
explain my mentality until I tell him what's on my mind. A
psychic hotline or visit to a psychic is useless because she
can't explain what I'm feeling or predict my future until I
provide her with enough information about me and issues
that I am dealing with in my life at that particular time. I
say all these things to say that only I can tell you about me,
and if I don't respect myself and believe in myself then I will
self destruct. The more I depend on an unseen supreme
force, the more I become out of character with self and that
takes me out of the independence status of being a man. I
speak of such issues that are preposterous to me and
detrimental as well. I write you in order for you to assist me
on my journey of truth. I know that at times you be tripping
on what I write or say but it's you my brother that ex-
panded my comprehension to a point where I'm not afraid
to question those in authority nor am I afraid to challenge
those that want to be in authority over my domain.

   My concern for your well being isn't unusual because I
worry about your health and state of awareness. If I had
your mind I could accomplish alot around here and in my
life. You are sharp and you are blessed with talent. Please
stay in shape with a fitness program and relax by listening
to a little jazz on your radio. Continue to write your book on
the "Montez Project" and continue to study for your Ph.D. I
love you and I brag about you as if you were a living legend
so represent your family. With Alex's financial skills and
your executive skills I know that when we all meet again
there's going to be some changes in this world. I lack the
skills that you both possess in business but my ideas and
determination will be worth contributing. I'm sorry if I didn't
answer any of your previous questions, please forgive me. I

look forward to your missives, responses, and words of wisdom. Peace and love to Che and Black Rose. I got much love for you. Stay strong and stay beautiful while you struggle...

Shalomluk/Wadu... your brother, Omar

Each day behind the wall, I learned more about me and the struggles of my people. I assumed that the best of our men were incarcerated because I had heard Black scholars say so. But after lengthy conversations and studying boys, who passed time *trade-watching*, I realized that our people were in serious trouble. We would undoubtedly perish as a people, if our well-being depended on the best of our thinkers being developed by europeanized institutions and anglo gulags. Our boys would need customary practices of Afrikanity that had not been defiled by eurocentric testing and approval.

Chapter 5- Love Aint...

Love threw me off the first year I was behind the wall. I cried and meditated. I tried prayer. I chanted mantras and attributes. I conversed with homeys about my emptiness, if I trusted them. I attempted to befriend love. I longed for love when I wasn't fighting the pungency created by ill-mannered boys or sensing the feint presence of my past. And yet, I remained in a state of pandemonium.

It had taken confinement for me to understand the significance of sharing with my loved ones how I felt. My timing was poor. How had my emotions been numbed? How had my love been devalued? Should I have imitated the anglo's love in order for my love to be recognized as love?

Prison had no place for love. Neither the head nor heart could contain love. So, in no way could the culturally popular place, detaining Amerika's mistakes, contain love. It did, however, hold love the way it detained everything. And if love was ever detected by individuals unfamiliar with the intense feeling, one would find survival more demanding than the need for love. Something about life in Amerika made love awkward, no doubt. But something in the funk seemed to obliterate love. Anyone reading my letters or answering my calls had every reason to question my caged 'love you(s)'. Eventually, my affection fell on deaf ears because my loved ones had been desensitized by having to do time with me.

May 2001

Dr. Moreno,

I send this letter with strength my brother because it's the most important. My love for you alone can't get you through the trenches. Che and Black Rose are the many reasons that I tolerate a lot of bullshit with these oppressors. Bruski's neighbor has twenty years and he has done 18 years 4 months on it. He went up before the people today 5/21/01 and was denied parole again. Bruski has seen worse cases than that but his neighbor is an individual that he's close to and they kick it daily. Shit like that is pain, fear, and strength that are mixed with anger and hate. I raise my right fist to my comrades- Che, Black Rose, Bruski. I have females from the past that are trying to re-enter my life but I have no time for re-lighting candles nor being manipulated by promises of money and sex. An uneducated weak bitch can't do shit for me but keep her distance.

Within the last 50 months I've had three women wanting to marry me and a fourth wanting to leave her husband for me. I'm serious my brother. They think I'm crazy for turning down their offers but they don't mean shit to me. I have female family members that are the women in my life and they are the only ones that have been riding with me through this drama. I don't deal with emotions nor let my dick head do my thinking.

I'm quite sure there are plenty waiting on me but they will be surprised at my decisions. I'm looking for more than a cheap thrill. Don't worry my brother because I have my mind on South American beauties and business minded queens.

I have the teacher's guide to the nuwaubic lessons that you sent me years ago. Remember? All I need is spanish, if you don't mind. My research sources here are zero so I am unable to research the subject and field of marketing food items. Just hold on to your recipes and I promise to obtain as much information as I can on marketing, in due time. Time is moving pretty fast and I have been going over all my paperwork from the past once again. I'm trying to tighten up on my skills and remain Universal. I'm still the most feared in discussions and debates and I'm known for throwing the whole kitchen sink at my opponents when I speak. I'm more quieter now and my mind are on better things besides arguing over info.

Continue to motivate and encourage Black Rose to write more speeches and I do look forward to seeing her and hearing her. Concentrate on your relationship with her and wash your hands with the past. Right now it's hard for me to concentrate on M.Y.R.A. and S.O.D. because my schedule is screwed up at the moment but as long as we all continue to think and bring ideas to the table we won't leave hungry. Stay strong and stay true to yourself and remember that I got much love for your and my family in the struggle.

I look forward to meeting your associates and representing you to the fullest...

Love Always,

Omar

Love encouraged Omar and me to live. We knew that our family needed us. The idea of an extended family became rhetorical as my blackness matured. Family didn't require blood to substantiate a kinship or bond in way of the Afrikan science.

Prison was the wrong place to define love with sexual misbehavior, but it was obvious that sex had males emoting themselves, when they should have been strengthening themselves to destroy a system which was methodically destroying any male identified as black – if his behavior indicated that he was not susceptible to the deviousness of what we termed as the system. I had to remind myself that control was not to be identified as strength as I watched the sissies manipulate the mainline (prison population) with their influence.

Chapter 6- As a People

Osi and I were like brothers the moment we met. From the looks of things - we were related. Same tribe. His family was Hausa. My family was, now, a diluted version of Hausa, Yoruba and Amerika. Still, the similarities were there.

Initially, Osi was intelligent. But prison corrupts. And corrupted negroes perpetuate ignorance, division, docility and self-hatred. Osi's misfortune was devastating. He'd been imprisoned without being a citizen and learned that Amerika exchanged breaths with Afrikans from throughout the Diaspora. However, no Afrikan was comparable to the Afrikan in Amerika preferring to be a negro. And sharing carbon dioxide was not to be mistaken as cuddling.

Osi became a hit man for the mentally challenged and called me out. They used him. His lean muscular physique was intimidating. His accent, confidence and intelligence made him special. The negroes didn't understand me. Hell, they didn't understand Osi, either. Yet, Osi was talkative and nice. The boys were obviously impressed with his accent. I was not accepting the restrictions of prison very well, but I appreciated battle. Battle seemed to lift me above the chaos. So, cancelling the brotherhood that existed between Osi and me was easy. Defeating him hand-to-hand was even easier. Learning that I had hurt a part of myself was the lesson that would take longer to learn than my broken rib would take to heal.

Twenty Fifth Day of June In The Two Thousand And One Year of Our Creator-EL KULUWM

My Dear Brother Dr. Moreno,

You are indeed the Sun of Righteousness and you have risen with healing in your wings. I send you peace and love and I pray that your soreness around your ribs are returning back to normal. I hadn't heard from you in a couple of weeks and I was very concerned about your well-being. When I don't hear from my family members after a certain period of time I get crazy thoughts going through my head. Your letters are nourishment for my soul and I have become dependent on receiving your wisdom just like a welfare recipient on the first of the month. We both have been busy but we both are steady growing under these abnormal circumstances. I thank you for the two pages of Spanish and for trying to make it as plain as possible for me. I'm steady building my vocabulary and so far so good. I have sent some of my old material to C'view along with letters and pictures that I have accumulated throughout my years in exile. I'm trying to narrow it down to only my Holy Tablets, Let's Set The Record Straight, Guerilla Financing, law material, and Spanish material. I'm a little rusty with my Nuwaubic because I've been concentrating more on things that I will be using on a daily basis, but I still review it and practice it from time to time. I'm ready to return in order to lend a hand to Ihsaan so we both can work systematically to free Che and Black Rose. I can only show my dedication to my comrades because nothing comes to a sleeper but dreams. If I'm not ready now, then I will never be. We have work to do and I'm ready to build with the tools I have obtained. Get well my brother and I pray that you heal properly. My thoughts are on my family and I have much love for you. Freedom today, tomorrow, freedom now and forever...

Omar-El

United – we, as a people, could be a force. And we know this. It is as natural as finding a seat in an auditorium one visits for the first time. No one has to tell you where to sit because you will sit where you are comfortable and the comfort is based on one's identity. Sure, there are exceptions to this rule. The exception is the negro. Of course, the negro wishes to offer opportunity to anyone and everyone (other than Blacks) just to prove that he is loving, different and considerate - despite maltreatment, mistreatment, unemployment, unjust laws targeting melanated persons, impoverished conditions, and cycles that preserve the anglo's dominance.

The negro will gladly take the anglo's *caca* just to prove to the anglo's god that he belongs in heaven.

Chapter 7- Temporary Presence

Nothing was off limits in our conversations. Omar was honest and I eventually regained my confidence and began to teach him without reservation. Besides, on mainline I was around all sorts of mentalities and they all tried to be heavy in some kind of way. They were heavy with religion, sports and politics – anything they could repeat from television viewing.

Few prisoners attempted to improve the conditions of prison. The inmates serving life sentences were the most complacent. Most inmates had just enough game or conversation to attract the affection of some sissy or some attention-starved guard.

I was different. Talk on the yard, cafeteria or barbershop wasn't sufficient for me. Repeating quotes from penitentiary *khutbahs* or sermons and the news did nothing to move me. I was only interested in the opinion or analysis of thinkers. I was concerned about solving the ills of my people and those interested in the plight of the disenfranchised.

As the penal system continued probing the lives of inmates and families, I knew that I was losing my complement. Makaarim, my most tender experience, was slipping away. Distance plus poor visibility minus hope times confusion divided by doubt equaled a devastated warrior.

Dreams, conversations and the silence of those hoping that I'd lose my wealth and family became factors verifying my suspicions. With my vision obstructed, my other senses became sharper. I had to use every word imaginable to emote myself and energize the recipient of my letters – male or female. Most prisoners wrote love letters, but my love required that I educate my people.

July 8, 2001

Dr. Moreno

  My brother, that is your job to tear your woman's weak foundation down and then rebuild her character and way of life with the truth. Continue to educate Black Rose and uplift her spirit. Constructive criticism is good for anyone. As far as your dream-insecurity is playing a major role in your life but I see no need for you to be insecure. The punk and the thugs represent enemies that are set out to destroy your hopes and dreams. The thugs are thieves that wanted your jewels (family). The 3 thugs and the 1 punk equals four and without knowledge of the four directions and four elements voodoo will destroy. You see, there must be four forces in unity to cast a powerful spell against a strong opponent. You represent strength and knowledge that's why you carried the stick and when you gave a fatal blow to one you depleted their shield and spell. The reason you were not emotional and didn't seem to care is because you were dead. You were there in the spirit form and because of your absence it was natural because children always seem to make contact with spiritual beings. Please understand that I'm not trying to scare you with such an interpretation but please analyze the situation, the relationship, and the dream… You are important to me and I need you as a part of my life. Yes, I can have the Spanish you send as long as it's in a letter form like before. I wrote two of the women Pinky and Marilyn, but I doubt they respond. I'm not good at writing letters but I gave it a try. I was honest with them and I explain my current situation in a corrupt system. Introduction letters are hard for me. I'm only good at responding. If you send anymore addresses I would appreciate a variety of women such as Caribbean, Hawaiian, Puerto Rican, Black, and etc. I learned not to question your purpose for giving me such an assignment but by being your student for many years now I feel that your reasons are beneficial to us both. I will continue to write the women that you send, but not all of them. When I touch down I would like to venture into some of Atlanta's intellectual,

Quran toting, career working, law abiding, spiritual black women. Why? because there are so many flavors when it comes to our Nubian sisters. Teach me how to communicate with such women. My Spanish is improving and I look forward to more phrases and conversation words. You are doing a great job with assisting me. I thank you. "Hannibal" is a good book because it allows you to enter the mind of the doctor's I just finished 'Pimp; The Story Of My Life' by Iceberg Slim. It's a true story so I made it my business to read it Bro, the last few years turned me into one hell of a book lover. Yes, according to the media in Alabama, males and females are being considered to shipping to out-of-state prisons due to Alabama's over crowdedness. There are 3,000 state inmates in county jails waiting to go to a camp. I just hope my comrades in the struggle receive some early release blessings. The picture of Sa'i is a few months old but he still looks strong and if you ever saw him in person you would be surprised at how he grew taller and put on a few pounds...

I love you and I pray that your ribs heal sooner than expected. Stay strong and stay true to yourself. Ra'iysa wrote me last week and I must admit that she's very intelligent and her handwriting is beautiful for her age. I love the lil gods and I will teach them well.

Shalomluk/Wadu,

-Omar-

My ribs wouldn't heal anytime soon. Undoubtedly, Osi and I would never speak to each other, again. Pride and strong ignorance kept us from breaking the barrier that negroes had constructed to maintain their comfort in a place that deserved destruction.

I fought to secure a position in Makaarim's heart and mind. Holding on to her was as difficult as not sweating in the oppressive heat. I had decided to focus on my studies, avoid becoming institutionalized and fortify my strengths.

July 15, 2001

Dr. Moreno,

No need to apologize for the lack of compositions because I know about the struggle and how things can get very hectic. A few weeks ago I had a confrontation with a nigga from Miami. He thought that just because he was 6'6" that he could run up on me and talk shit. I let him talk shit for a minute until I finally stood up and checked his punk ass and then niggas started grabbing me to hold me back. All I demand is respect, not love from these weak, sex craving, ass kissing, snitching ass, want to be thugs. I stay in shape for reasons such as these.

Your last missive dealing with the Deity Ra or "Re" was superb and and I loved the way you kicked it to me. You gave me degrees to add on to my weakest points and links and anytime a person causes me to go back to the holy scriptures I can't do anything but show my respect, and you deserve my respect and admiration. You covered some familiar ground but you went more in detail and history and that's what I love. Bro, don't ever think that I can't compre-hend your teachings because I'm no more than a reflection of you, so don't ever hold back. Religion and Spirituality are my strongest points and thanks to you, I'm getting only stronger.

As far as Ihsaan, you are right, we can't lose him to the oppressors and we won't. I just need a little more time to get there in order to be his shadow. I dedicate my life to our prosperity, struggle, and repairment. Bro, if I return to

C'view and don't make a change for the better of our family then my time in exile was done in vain and wasted entirely. I have Chelsea trying to locate my "lil bro" down south because he and I lost contact a few years ago became of modern day slave kkkolonies. I taught him at Lancaster and he thinks highly of me and my ideas. You see, I don't play chess but I'm still making moves for my own.

I love you and I remain forever your brother, friend, and student.

Shalomluk/Wadu,

Omar Sa'i

Games! Regardless of the position we take on an issue, we have been subjected to a contest that will eventually require skill whether we recognize the rules, commit to playing or realize that the game requires a hustler's mentality. Meaning – you have to be aggressive. Besides, Amerika does not care if you have talent or not... when she dispatches her troops. At this point, chess is no longer a game.

JULY 30, 2001

DR. MORENO,

PEACE MY BROTHER AND I PRAY THAT ALL IS WELL. I'M PROUD OF YOU FOR STRIVING TOWARDS YOUR PH.D AND I'M OVERWHELMED WITH JOY THAT YOU ARE MORE THAN CLOSE TO RECEIVING IT. DON'T WORRY ABOUT OWING ME LETTERS BECAUSE YOU NEVER WILL OWE ME ANYTHING. I'M FOREVER IN YOUR DEBT AND WILL FOREVER ASSIST AND PROTECT YOU. I'M SORT OF UPSET BECAUSE I'M NOT IN RECEIPT OF KIJANA'S LETTER THAT'S WRITTEN IN RED

INK. I BELIEVE THEY HAVE TAMPERED WITH MY MAIL OR I'M JUST BEING IMPATIENT. IF I RECEIVE IT I WILL INFORM YOU IMMEDIATELY. BUT I AM IN RECEIPT OF THE APPLICATION AND KHALIFAH'S ACCESSORY PRODUCTS PRICE LIST. IN DUE TIME I WILL APPLY BUT FOR NOW I CAN'T AFFORD TO PAY THE REGISTRATION FEE NOR PUT A STRAIN ON MY FAMILY POCKETS. I'M FINE AT THE MOMENT AND I'M TRYING NOT TO ORDER ANY KIND OF MATERIAL BECAUSE I'M MAKING PREPARATIONS TO DEPART. LAST MONTH I CLEANED UP AROUND MY HOUSE IN ORDER TO PERPARE FOR RELOCATION. I MUST KEEP IT LIGHT. I HAVE ALSO BLESSED INDIVIDUALS WITH MATERIAL IN ORDER TO HELP THEIR GROWTH. I THINK OF CHE AND BLACK ROSE AND THEIR WELL-BEING MORE THAN I DO ANYONE ELSE. IF THEY ARE BEING PROPERLY PROVIDED FOR, THEN I'M SATISFIED. AS FAR AS MY SPANISH IS GOING, I'M NOT DOING SO GOOD AT THE MOMENT. I STILL KICK IT WITH MY MEXICAN PARTNER WHENEVER I SEE HIM BUT SOMETIMES I GET FRUSTRATED AND CONFUSED. THERE'S SO MUCH GOING ON MY WAY THAT I'M LOOKING FOR AN EARLY SURPRISE. AUGUST IS A CRUCIAL MONTH FOR THE STATE BECAUSE DEADLINES MUST BE MET AND THEIR BUDGET IS LOW, SO YOU CAN IMAGINE WHAT STATE OF MIND I'M IN. ABOUT THE DREAM…I MEANT NO HARM WHEN I MENTIONED DEATH. I JUST GAVE MY INTERPRETATION AND EXPRESSED MY VIEW. YOU HAVE A LOT TO LIVE FOR AND WE ALL WILL OUT LIVE A BUNCH OF SUCKERS. I WISH YOU WELL WITH YOUR MARRIAGE AND I CAN'T SEE IT NO OTHER WAY. ENCLOSED WITH THIS LETTER IS THE 'COMMUNIST MANIFESTO' AND I'M HONORED TO ASSIST YOU…I GOT MUCH LOVE FOR YOU AND WILL NEVER LET ME DOWN.

SHALOMLUK/WADU,

OMAR

I had lived a good life. Still, I was straining to keep my head up, gain momentum, and outlive the hate that was bruising my chest. I couldn't fathom how anyone labeled a 'have not' handled all the crap capable of being shoveled on the downtrodden.

I would like to think that my being behind the wall – *adentro* – was my fault, but the mandatory minimums, social perception, public indoctrination, and other mechanisms of programming and propaganda assured me that I was wrong to fault myself. Amerika needed to know that she was just as *wrong*. Like two left shoes.

Chapter 8- Diminishing Differences

Alex and I met James Stevenson while in federal custody in Needles, California. He was a young, bright brotha out of Los Angeles with roots in Arkansas. Alex stayed in touch with him and supported him from May of '99 until losing contact in 2006. This was after their confrontation and Stevenson's initial attempt to advise us on surviving prison.

The brotha meant well, but Alex hadn't fixated on the end nor the damages mounting on my freedom. I had to return him to our families regardless of my naïveté and chances of seeing the streets, again. I took a hit and got Alex's charges dropped. I was headed to one of Amerika's worst penal systems. All of them are disastrous, but some have educed and/or conjured monsters at a faster rate than others. So, I listened to Stevenson. Hell, I was scared, confused and wondering how this aspect of California living, *Colors* or *American Me* had escaped me. I missed the beaches, smell of strawberries, the girls, people jogging, biking and rollerblading.

Eventually, I heard from Stevenson. I used my letters to awaken his indwelling intelligence. I enjoyed his poetry, appreciation for learning and literature. His letters were reminiscent of Omar's growth. It was remarkable to see how he'd matured as a man, embraced fatherhood and come to respect women. His impression of me caused him to speak freely of me. Granted, I was different; I didn't try to be. Of course, he shared my existence with others who'd fallen and decided to stand up and speak out. As a result, I got more letters from other inmates.

Kijana Mtume Allah-El was one of the sharpest minds at Tehachapi, if not in the bowels of California and therefore, Amerika. Despite the presence of wealthy murderers, baffled children of mega-stars or notorious thugs, Kijana was serious about giving back to the community. I shared his information with Omar. And for awhile, we were able to build through our mail network. My teachings, beliefs or thoughts about the Five Percent Nation were of little concern as I grew and saw that in the years to come... Amerika would have a problem with melanated youth. And if the melanated youth continued to ignore their legacy and share freely with disadvantaged white kids, Amerika would lose a number of them to the plight of my people or we'd find ourselves with a generation of lost, listless, digitally influenced, indifferent negroes.

August 2, 2001 3L9

Dr. Moreno,

 After reading Kijana's missive and seeing how the brother wants to build with you, I felt blessed for being your student and for knowing you better than the next man. Brothers reaching out to meet you and learn from you is indeed a great honor but seeing 'gods of the earth' acknowledging that you are a "child of the Eloheem", is what I consider to be a prophecy fulfilled. I was able to relate to Kijana and flow along with his supreme mathematics and I must give him credit for representing for all five percenters. His ideas are similar to ours as far as helping the youth and turning P.O.W letters into a book for the conscious readers. Remember I mentioned earlier about our letters are history? I like his style and it would be an honor to meet him and converse on a god-like vibe and build.

 I would like to inform you that the letter in red ink brought me heat along with the background in the photo. Drawings and addresses are detrimental in my environment and 'blue eyes' see such things as being gang related. My honesty, eye contact, and representation of the Moors saved me. We must continue to use black ink dipped in blood but never red or blue. People fear what they don't understand nor conquer so continue with the esoteric teachings. In the future, I will use Nuwaubic when on the phone or talking to S.O.D. about plans, places, and people. I need to tighten up my skills in order to contribute to my family. From here on out we must discontinue the use of addresses, numbers, and drawings on our missives. I mean no harm and my intentions are good. Continue studying for your PH.D and congratulations on 'hard work paying off'. We must free Che, Black Rose, Sa'i, and brothers like Kijana because they are missing in action and we could use their determination to live in peace. I got much love for you and I look forward to the day that we meet again...

Shalomluk/Wadu,

Omar

The time would come when I would sit and build with Kijana's brothers and sisters; Gods of the Earth. I truly hoped that I would not be so poor that they would overlook the righteousness of my teachings or the direction of my conviction. In Amerika, success is capable of selling the most harmful of products and ideas. More importantly, I wanted my self-evaluations to ascertain that I had questioned my lessons and advanced with the most simplistic explanation of the conundrums that seem to captivate, confound and conquer the masses.

Chapter 9 - Struggling with Struggle

One of the most appreciative aspects of blackness is struggle. I am convinced that success for a Black person is the pinnacle of success, for blackness attracts obstacles which cause one to endure far more than any anglo ever endures.

By no means, would I ever equate slavery to the struggle that I speak of, but I can't dismiss slavery when I speak of struggle because it is obvious that the experience of slavery altered the DNA of my people and contributed to every problem that we experience as a group, today. Not many of us wanted change in those days and a many of us are complacent with slavery in these days.

September 18, 2001

Dr. Moreno,

I'm in the middle of Alex Haley's "Queen" and so far it's the best book I've read this year because it deals with slavery in the South and I can relate. I never read a book that makes me dream like "Queen" has been doing. Yes, I actually become characters from the book in my dreams and I never have experienced such an effect on my mental until I opened "Queen". It speaks of freedom but the slaves don't really want it because they are content and too lazy to be independent, and I can relate because I see it often on the modern day slave plantations. Negroes get comfortable and sell each other out for free- world sandwiches or items off of the canteen. I mention this book to mention that I will not allow Che, Black Rose, or Sa'i to become content like the characters in this book nor allow them to give up on the most beautiful thing, which is "struggle".

I pray to our Creator that you are in the best of health and I send strength for you while you are in the trenches. I often speak of struggle and liberation because they go hand in hand, and there's nothing more I could wish for at this moment but your freedom. I feel it, I smell it, and you are so close now that we both can grasp it. An educated brother like yourself brings smiles to my face because I'm honored to be a part of your education. The letter you wrote for me, concerning my transformation, made my eyes watery and I woke up at 4a.m. before work and re-read your kind words and once again, watery eyes. To be honest, I never knew you were that proud of your lil' bro. I thank you for your honesty, kind words, and love for me. Your gift for organizing words and making a statement are what I consider to be an extraordinary gift that has been bestowed upon you only by the 'Eloheem". I'm serious man, you are blessed. As far as your PhD, I look forward to seeing that degree of achievement hanging in your office.

One of the questions you asked did I care for my mental, physical, and spiritual while in exile, and my answer to you is a positively yes. I'm in the best shape of my life and I feel good about myself these days. Thanks to you, I was able to sit and debate with the so-called best scholars and go more in depth with every issue that was ever mentioned. The old me would've looked like a chump in front of them so-called best. Don't you know that I haven't debated or argued in two month? I chose to chill out with religious and political issues. I'm surrounded by so many Negroes that recommend that Amerikkka go to Afghanistan and bomb it off the map. Others suggest that they capture and execute 'Osama Bin Laden' for being a prime suspect in the 9/11/01 bombing and hijacking. I'm tired of listening to these old niggas that fought in Vietnam also on what they think. Vietnam veterans are weak mothafuckas that got slaughtered by a bunch of women dressed in uniform that was dedicated and devoted to their men and homeland, enough to fight for a good cause. That's right, Vietnamese women helped fight in the jungle. Now those women are what you call "Ride or Die Women"! Niggas always talking about they want a "Ride or

Die Bitch", but how many black bitches are down for their man? How many black bitches will die for their nigga? My opinion of Amerikkka is obvious and my opinion of Osama Bin Laden is that I hope Allah guide, protect, and continue to avenge him and his people. I send peace to you my brother and it was good to hear from you once again. My love for Che, Makaarim, & Sa'I is stronger than ever and my love for you as well. Thanks for the Spanish page. We will meet again...

Shalomluk/Wadu,

Omar

Yeah, slavery did a job on us. Be it the English or the Arabs – oppression is oppression. And I shouldn't have to take sides or fight wars that I will not benefit from. Countless brown and black children sacrifice their lives for what we call livelihood. It can't be freedom. It has to be to make a living at the expense of others dying. Actually, few ever contemplate that our war is not offshore, but on the shores that we built. Amerika has to know that she owes us. She should never sleep. She should toss and turn at any attempt because she has abandoned the very people who structured her with their talent, intelligence, endurance, sacrifice, compassion and ignorance.

September 23, 2001

Dr. Moreno,

It's funny and strange how Ihsaan's situation is similar to mines. The only difference is that I'm not married now, thanks to you. We both took married women from their punk ass husbands and we both fell in the trap of a ready-

made family. We both did more for the women's children and family members, more than we did for our own family members. My woman broke me and took me through some changes but I'm thankful because there isn't a whore on earth that can play under me again. I care less about a bitch and I pray that our brother learn from experience and move on with his life because there are so many different flavors of women and it's time that he try a new exotic flavor. As far as 'Nean saying that she's tired of me calling her house, she's a liar because I hardly use the phone, it's very rare.

I send peace to you and I hope all is well. I didn't pick up this pen to stress you out about problems in the family. My primary purpose is to discuss you and I, our struggle, our search for peace, and our reunion. I try to concentrate on Che, Black Rose, and Sa'i because of their present living conditions and hopefully they will return to help the rest of the family. I wish I had your skills of writing. Indeed, your letters captivate, inspire, and motivate me every time, and I can imagine the effect your pen has on women. Throughout the years I have managed to touch and change women ideas and opinions, but never their lives like you have. I think my sense of humor interferes with women's views of me, and average black man incapable of being serious. A woman never has acknowledged me as being a "God", I guess because I never know that I was capable of being one. Please don't misunderstand me, I never had a problem with meeting and sleeping with women. I just got a problem with meeting a "lady". I wasn't blessed with a big dick nor a long tongue, but blessed with the ability to fulfill their every freaky fantasy, sexually. That shit is worthless and meaningless to me now because I see sex differently now, and I feel that if I can't sex a woman mentally before sexually then I'm half a man. It's hard to believe but niggas actually laugh at Sa'i because no female attempts to visit him. They think he's lame with weak game, but little do they know about Sa'i. I respect him because he listened to you and he got rid of hoes in his life in order to prepare for what awaits him. Sa'i claims that if I see the women that come visit these niggas I would laugh in disgust. Those niggas brag of their "top-notch hoes" but when you see them they look like shit with their gold teeth and fake Versace outfits. It seems that women in Alabama love to stuff their faces at the table with tasty meats from the swine because 8 out of 10 are fat. I think we will all be proud of Sa'i's new mentality. On one of your missives you mentioned that you couldn't wait to meet my wife, and that statement touched me and made me simile because I know good things awaits me. Dr. Moreno, my heart longs for a decent conversation with a woman and my body aches for the scent and touch of a woman. I am stronger and never weaker I know now what it takes to satisfy one mentally, physically and spiritually. I now know the true meaning of "soul mate".

I'm still reading Alex Haley's "Queen" and the book is pretty tight. Once again I thank you for the Spanish words. I'm excited about learning those new words and phrases. Please keep sending words like that. I must tighten up on my skills within these last three months of the year. I'm pretty sure I will impress you. I thank you for writing that letter for me concerning my life. I appreciate everything you do for me. The drawing of you is very artistic and you are a handsome dude. I'm proud of your progress and the positive influence you have on people you encounter. I wish you well in the kkkourts and I pray that you remain forever that "Supreme Being" that you represent. Peace and love to the family, Che, Makaarim and Sa'i. Stay strong and continue to earn your degree. Your dreams of the islands and beaches will soon be a reality as long as we keep breathing.

Shalomluk/Wadu,

Omar

Amerika has hurt those resembling me in so many ways. Most say that we have access to an education, jobs, and things that an education and job are supposed to bring. That isn't enough when we consider that we are rarely celebrated by us; unless you consider self-hatred something to ceremonialize. And when we do choose to uplift and love us, we are accused of reverse racism, bigotry, prejudice, supremacy and of course, ancestral worship.

Everything I wish to do without the consent of the anglo - the *yurugu* - I am criticized for. Unfortunately, the negro feels the pain of his master, after a cowardly critique, and publicly slams any Afrikan willing to stand as a man.

Nonetheless, I pursued a degree and I understood why my brother and other inmates were encouraging me to capture a piece of the anglo as if I hadn't got enough from public schooling, TV, and making purchases. I confess that such an attainment was a fraction of compartmentalized data. I'd have to listen to my Elders and acknowledge my Ancestors in order to appreciate the sciences as they were intended. However, they did not know that Amerika was developing a new pool of menial laborers for purposes of servicing and serving. Prison was creating an entirely new minority. Now, non-white felons would also have issues that would make being black or brown – an uglier thing.

Chapter 10- A Branch of Evil

I would think that I have never had a problem that money couldn't solve. Though, I am certain that I solved a many without money. Amerika is a capitalistic country and Amerika runs on capital. So, appealing to Amerika without enough capital would be similar to having clips of ammunition without firearms. Easily, I admit - I am not that thrilled about experiencing hardship. And despite our struggles – a lot of us would rather have it easy. Somehow, we have been robbed of the drive that made us architects, mathematicians, educators, alchemists, hunters, physicians, warriors, thinkers, scribes, providers and protectors...by those that we habitually and ignorantly embrace.

October 16, 2001

Dr. Moreno,

I hope and pray that you are feeling better this week. This is "flu" season so be careful and remain physically strong by maintaining a healthy diet. I need you home in the best condition possible. If I could take our place I would because I know that you are the positive type of brother that society and the struggle needs and awaits. You are a Messiah and don't even know it! You surprised me when you mentioned that you weren't sure of my mind set when I return home. Well, out of all people it's you that knows my true potential, capabilities, and future plans but no man knows my fate. To be honest with you, mind is set on money as soon as I get some fresh air and after that then and only then will I be able to breathe. I have plenty of plans but without "capital" I cannot initiate one. Alex does the best he can for us and I want to help him to help us all with legal matters. I know for a fact that my assistance will be quite beneficial. I have a friend in Dade city, Florida that I consider to be my lil bro. From '92-'96 I took care of him while he was in the trenches and our reunion awaits the two of us. I made contact a couple of months ago and it seems that he has become quite fond of my family. Our family has embraced him as a family member through letters and that means a lot to me. Step#1 is into play and step #2 is in the game. While niggas be sleeping, I be up plotting and scheming! If you're going to believe in something, then believe in me. I won't let you down and Mentors Yielding Roots Abroad won't let us down. All you must do is prepare to take your rightful place at the throne. At first I disagreed with such leadership but now my foresight allows me to respect what I see. I respect you, I miss you, and I love you. If you have doubts about my mind set, then you have doubts about G-O-D...

Shalomluk,
Omar

After experiencing the mentality of a hustler, one has an idea of whether or not someone will hustle in the wrong way. My degree would be worthless after prison. My skin would become more noticeable. And if I was religious, I'd always be honest with white folk. Simple! After all, I was supposed to be one of the mis-educated negroes with a double minority status.

Zip codes, expensive clothes, shiny cars, and trophy women were supposed to define me or broadcast my success. My Ancestors had me against the ropes. Some of them were choking me because I was contemplating suicide most days. The message was clear... I would not be successful doing what I thought was good for me, but what was good for our people. Creativity, self-sufficiency – you know... the stuff that you don't think of in a recession. I needed that nudge to get me going because prison did more damage than I showed. I wasn't raped, shanked or beaten. I didn't participate in any non-Nubian sexual activity. I certainly didn't encourage any sexual misbehavior, either. Still, the environment was disastrous. My personal *jihad* was the type of struggle that made death more appealing.

October 28, 2001

Dr. Moreno,

Peace unto you my strong Nubian brother. We struggle in the trenches together and I send you strength to carry on. I received your two missives and I thank you for the inspiration and for believing in me. Your hope for me being productive isn't strange to me because there are others that are waiting to see what I'm going to do. My character and behavior will shock a lot of people because whatever they're expecting I'm going to give them the opposite. No one will ever pick my brain to see what I'm thinking and as far as trust, I must take my time to earn it by others and for me to accept others into my world. Ihsaan is my main priority because he kept this family together and I must pay my dues by doing whatever it takes to assist a brother in need. He still has hope for Moreno-Brown Entertainment and if we have to drop an EP to attract clients and fans then I'm willing to hit the studio. I still love music and throughout the years I have created enough music ideas to help finance MBE for a long time. I would like to do a single with Gravity for business purposes only. Other than that, I have plans with a few comrades that could help build S.O.D. I informed Ihsaan that I'm anxious to help with legal matters concerning Black Rose and Che; that would start the moment I breathe some fresh air again. I will never turn my back on those that have struggled with me and struggled for me. Always remember that!!! Bro, I'm no longer afraid. My only concern is longevity and if I'm going to last I know that I need you by my side.

I finished "Queen" a couple of weeks ago along with Sidney Sheldon's "Nothing Lasts Forever". I also got a chance not to read in entirety but flip through a few pages of Dr. Ronn Elmore's "How to Love a Black Woman". I stay busy reading and studying just to cover a lot of issues that people normally discuss. I can't wait to fill up my bookshelf with books by black authors and of course, Sheldon and Grisham books. I'm proud to hear that your studies are going well and that your dissertation will soon be completed. I look forward to reading your novel. Whatever happened to the "Montez Project"? You never mention it anymore and I just wanted to know the outcome. One day you and I could collaborate on a "fiction" about three Nubians going though the penal system in the South and returning to society with success stories. I once tried to work on creating a "board game" dealing with life issues but I gave up because it got to complicated. It dealt with peoples transformations through difficult experiences in life. I try to think of things that people haven't thought of yet. I'm trying to be more creative, like with the idea of M.Y.R.A. I often sit and think about managing three strippers throughout the South. I talked to a guy back in '99 from Auburn, AL and he hipped me to his nieces that would love to come to Florida to work under my management. Their dreams are to strip and leave Alabama. I kick it with a guy out of Evergreen that moved to Pensacola in the '90's and he used to strip in P'cola. He's in excellent shape and we have been working out together for years, we met in '98. He wants to strip again and I told him I could hook him up with an opportunity if he allows me to be his manager. I also hooked up with two rappers out of Mobile and I would like to produce an album for them. They are tight and they listen to my advice about the music business. I still read up on the newest equipment and what sounds are selling. You see, I be busy promoting MBE, I'm just waiting to see better days.

Speaking of strippers, I know our lil sis is engaged to one but I can't control her decisions. I love Danielle and I care about her well-being and my disapproval of a ten-year difference cannot be used to interfere in her love life. Experience is the best teacher! Everytime I tell her that I have plans for her and that she will have plenty of money with my assistance, she laughs at me. Yes, she laughs at me everytime because she doesn't believe in me but it's cool though. I wanted to make her a leader of a S.O.D. branch because I saw the potential and fire in her eyes. Danielle has a serious look on her face everytime I see her but when she smiles she lights up the whole room. Her characteristic is "dangerous" and that's what I like about her. All these years I had planned to teach and use her as a leader because I thought she looked up to me, but I was wrong. Just like you taught your lil bro, that's how I wanted to teach my lil sis. I wanted someone to look up to me for guidance but at the same time I have a child (ren), nieces, and nephews that I must invest my time and energy into. Danielle wrote me and surprised me with her engagement last week and I responded with 'best wishes" because I know how sensitive she is whenever I speak harsh words, I just told her that I will not tolerate "domestic violence" towards my lil sis nor any of my sisters. I will punish a nigga that physically abuse my sister and I mean that.

I thank you for mentioning my son (Brient) in New York somewhere and I really appreciate that. That incident took me through some changes but I'm more mature now, and I have no more excuses for my failures. I have plans for Ian, Ihsaan, Malaysia, and Ra'iysa and whenever I get on my feet I will pay Brandy a visit to check on her children. I hold no grudges but I have leaned to keep my distance and let everyone live their lives.

I love you big bro and if possible, I would like for you to put me on your visiting list at the end of this year. If Anu allows me to see a better day then I promise that I'm coming to see you... I love you.

Shalomluk/Wadu, Omar

Often, I am surprised by people who know of no one in prison. C'mon! This is Amerika! Amerika is a prison state, narco-state. Look! It ain't hard to do time in Amerika. *You can get it!* Enslaved black skin is a commodity.

Omar visited me, while I was in prison. I knew that we would see each other, again. My mom, Alex, Daniela, Chelsea, Omari (nephew) and Barron (brother-in-law) assembled to see us all together for the first time in many years. It was a painful visit. I hated visits. The idea of stripping naked after being recharged by your family was emasculating. Stripping before a visit was tough enough because you were about to touch your loved ones. So much damn nudity! No doubt, the sexually aggressive style of the anglo was facilitated by the penal system. I was ruined by the madness. It would take a year for me to be comfortable being naked once I left the punk factory.

With the anal fascination, sexual drugs to prolong erections or numb one's throat, and toys to know one's self in the most inappropriate ways, I was intimidated and sex seemed much more aggressive and painful than I had remembered.

Chapter 11- Fast Forward

As I prepared to leave prison, I was confident. Belief that I had familial and financial support enabled me to walk through the doors, but I wasn't sure about my conflict resolution skills outside a tactical environment. I found myself recognizing that success and peace for my people would have to be a collective effort. It was impressive to see Nubians working towards building a nation but division retarded the efforts because we fail to prepare for disagreements that we will have as a people or group. This fact makes it tough for us to become a nation.

Life behind the wall had hardened me for my own survival. Yet, there was a part of me that refused to violate the wishes of anyone. Unless that individual intended me physical harm. I had become so physically aggressive that Yoga kept me cool, *dhikr*(ing) (chanting) the remembrance of the Creator calmed me and the fact that no one was listening humbled me. I had changed from being selfish to focusing on my behavior as a Nubian. I no longer needed to be validated by material possessions fashioned by the oppressor. Neither did I feel the need to quote anglo scholars without recognizing legacy of brilliant Black minds.

November 2002

Dr. Moreno,

Peace unto you my dear brother. You always give me hope. I don't have a low self-esteem but sometimes it's good for the soul to hear encouraging words from others that have experienced what I have. I thank you and I will forever have you in my life as a brother, friend and mentor. On 11/10/02 Yvonnia, Bramun, and Napeitre paid Sai a visit. After receiving several letters in the month of October from an apologetic woman, it convinced him that it was time to talk. He took your advice and Chelsea's as well. As soon as he submitted the new visiting list and informed her of the approval, she came. The children acted as if he had never left their lives because they were all on him. They embraced him and one by one they spoke of how they missed him; they shared their lives; and remembered him as a positive father figure. He was impressed on their remembrance of events he never thought they would remember. He listened attentively as they opened up their lives to him. Sa'i joked, played and gave advice. He even help Napeitre with a lil' Spanish because she has taken a couple of classes. Even Bramun spoke a few words very clearly. About Yvonnia... the conversation remained friendly and she was treated as a friend. A lot of issues weren't discussed with the 21/2 hours but in due time they will be. He asked about Che's missive and her answer for not writing back was, "I don't know, I just didn't because I don't know how." She was afraid that the question came up because she trembled and dropped her head. Sa'i didn't pursue any farther with the questioning of Che's missive, instead he moved to a different area of questioning. He kept her comfortable but nervous at the same time. The children felt and saw the tension but Sa'i's sense of humor kept things going. Bro, when I was time to go she hugged Sa'i, kissed him, held him , and told him how much she cared for him. He didn't get emotional and to his surprise he didn't even get aroused. Yes, it's been a long time since he touched a woman but he honestly admits that he didn't feel those natural vibes between man and woman. He laid in his rack and questioned himself. I truly believe that if Sa'i wasn't spiritually centered that he would've let his emotions make decisions for him. I'm proud of him for representing strength but I'm puzzled with his feeling. I love Sa'i, Che, and Makaarim and if people don't have their best interest in mind then they are against their struggle. I can't and I won't try to convince individuals to like me nor anyone else, but those that insist on being my comrades' enemies then my comrades' enemies are my enemies. In due time Sai will *finish his interrogation. He didn't try to run game on her nor make any promises. He handled himself real well and he represented everything that he stands firm on. He left a positive impression on her and her children.*

Dr. Moreno, I can honestly say that Sa'i is ready. I pray that Che maintains his sanity. His day in November is coming. I wish him well when he touches down. I love you always and I send peace and love to Black Rose, Che and Sa'i. Thanks for listening to my plans...

Shalomluk/Wadu,

Omar

The stories of Geronimo Pratt and George Jackson inspired me because their stories depicted the diabolical intentions of the government. Therefore, if a brotha is fighting for his people, without authorization from the government or without hedging, said brotha understands the dangers of utilizing the limited powers of the 1st Amendment. More importantly, we must not betray our Ancestors in the process of struggling to better the conditions of our people. And too, the answers to our problems lie within the confines of blackness opposed to the generosity of our oppressor.

November 2002

Dr. Moreno,

Time stops for no man. I say that to say that time is flying and soon a change will come. My thoughts are on the month and Che. I get nervous at times but I'm anxious and excited. It's sad to say but I can honestly speak on Sai's behalf. Sai is not a fighter and he doesn't he doesn't intend on doing no more than 7 years. After the seven year mark, either way it goes I truly believe that he will move on to a better place. Some say that the number seven is completion, but according to my opinions it's number nine. I must agree with the scholars on 7 this time because it sounds better for me and Sai. I must agree that it takes more than prayer and sore knees to change the hearts of Che, Black Rose, and Sai's oppressors. When Che and black rose are liberated I know that they will reach out and grab their comrade. Geronimo Pratt used to write my partner Michael Kimble "Najee". Remember the brother you wrote questioning you about the Akdar group and its practices? He was affiliated with BPP and BLA, so he say. In prison you can become anyone and leave out being anything. He introduced me to the Black Movement era and revolutionary views. We all meet great teaches along the way and I must say that he wasn't a great teacher but he opened my eyes to a new world of thinking. If Sai grasp life lessons like I did, I guarantee he will be a deep brother that will be hard to handle. I'm a strong believer in fate and I truly believe that it was meant for me to meet some of them "brothers of the struggle" deep off in the trenches.

I thank you for sharing the greatest secret in the world. I truly overstand. I like I mentioned in previous missives, I'm not afraid to neither lead nor be led. I have leadership potential but I rather listen and learn this time from someone with experience. I'm tired of being poor giving up on success. I'm ready more than ever. S.O.D. means a lot to me so I can't stop and I won't stop. I won't give up and never give in. Everything you have shared with me for the last five years will eventually pay off in the long run. This might sound funny but I always wanted a lil brother to teach just like you taught me. You see, for years I have tried to drill Danielle and teach her. I used to make attempts to reach out to her like you did me. I failed in some ways because she is a female and it was kind of harder for me. She loves me and respects me dearly, and she does listen but her comprehension is a different story. Bro, don't you know that LaFreda wrote me and asked for a favor? She asked me to write her 13 year old daughter "Sequoia" because peer pressure was getting the best of her. I was shocked and surprised but honored that she actually believed that there is something that I could share with her daughter. I wrote her a two page letter and I hope that my letter makes a difference. It's a start for me but a giant leap for M.Y.R.A. because that's exactly what it's about – reaching out and uplifting the Nubian youth. My letter might not affect Sequoia's life but it's a major step for me and my friendship with her and her mother. I thought I would share that with you because it's you who inspires me to touch lives with paper and pen. The pen is my voice and hopefully my voice will get louder as the ink flows. I love you big bro.

Shalomluk/Wadu,

Omar

When I started teaching Omar I didn't assume that I'd ever need him to teach me anything. I can't be certain of why I helped my brother and several other inmates, but I am glad that I helped Bruce Omar Brown. Perhaps, I was selfish. Of course, I knew that despite my loneliness – we are never alone. Therefore, Afrikans in Amerika must make grabbing and railroading our children much tougher. And trusting their safe return to a system of destruction is erroneous. Faith based programs, a G.E.D. and mandated classes ordered by the department of corrections will not prepare our sons, fathers and brothers for the cold world that awaits them. And we should not allow Afrikan males to entertain returning to our communities diseased and weakened by dissexual misconduct. Nor should they come home afraid to be men. If properly nurtured, *enkhemeticized* (enblackened) and educated in an Afrikan manner, we can expect to effectively utilize this captivity to identify and extract the warrior.

Extracting the Warrior

After Thoughts

The anglo's history records that Afrikans were brought to the Virginia colony of Jamestown in British North America in 1619 for the purpose of enslavement. The Afrikans in question were not slaves. And no question about it - they had to be *enslaved*. And today, many of us are being enslaved.

The 13th Amendment and greed has made the continued enslavement of melanated people feasible. And of course, enslaving the builders and maintainers of Amerika makes enslaving every citizen easier. Not everyone is subjected to physical enslavement because tax slaves are more abundant. Moreover, the forced migration of Afrikans could never be confused with population transfer because the migration was involuntary. And after enduring slavery, Jim Crowism, the Negro Revolution, the Black Movement and all the revolutions that haven't been televised, we show more compassion to our oppressors than we show love to ourselves. No doubt, we suffer from the *Stockholm Syndrome.* Somehow, we identify with our captors and see their problems as our own. We sympathize with a people who dare not to empathize with us. We make excuses for the slave masters and condemn our Ancestors who subjected us to slavery. Yeah, some of our people expected compassion from foreigners who were unfamiliar with compassion. Still, we survive dog attacks, church bombings, and suppression by water hose, police brutality, and imposed poverty, segregation, prejudice, racism, and bigotry, bias based on appearance and anything else that one can bring to us or throw at us. We endure it all. Yet, when we fight back or speak out, negroes want to whisper and translate the intended message to their bedroom buddies.

I hope the enclosed letters written by Omar Sa'i gives you an urgency to visit courtrooms; ready lists of skilled, caring attorneys with a proven record; decide to redefine success; extend family; and embrace blackness.

As the country struggles economically, under-employment, unemployment, impoverishment and all that accompanies poverty is accepted as the fault of disenfranchised individuals who have depended on their oppressor to make them equal, after trusting negroes who assembled behind closed doors to reason that cooperation and loyalty was the most effective means to gaining the compassion of a people who had once treated us like animals. Few would ever blame the economy for the decisions made by individuals elected to destroy the structure of this country.

We refuse to see how we've been victimized because the *Talented Tenth* constantly reminds us that we are not to blame the anglo for our ills. Surely, blaming the anglo is *not* the solution, but identifying the culprit is necessary if we expect to ever move beyond our obstacles.

The selected self-serving leaders of the African-American communities and anglo lap dogs refuse to address post-slavery trauma because they feel that their personal love for the anglo male should be adopted globally. In public, they cry of the perils associated with being Black, but behind closed doors they bare the phallus of their masters and gratefully take position on all fours with their mouths wide open. More amazing is the fact, that they want us to pretend that we don't know that they have sold-out for the *bitch* role or a *kept* role. Furthermore, they lose time trying to teach their spouse, children, congregation, delegation and/or community the meaning of respect. Their mentioning of historic racial wrongs or the upliftment of Black folks is bogus. They say enough to appease common negroes and simultaneously incite black males working within the system, with a militant undertone. Said leaders are dangerous because they talk tough and solicit funds from the people they speak of opposing. In essence, their efforts and battles are financed by their secret lovers. This being said, one shouldn't expect much from this particular type of negro... if one is to trust any negro.

The anglo will never understand how we can speak of the numerous historical, diabolical transgressions committed against Nubians and what such treatment entitles us to. Yet, they feign ignorance when recognizing the unfair economic, social, militaristic, and psychological advantage they have due to their ancestors.

Undoubtedly, something about being Black, in Amerika, has sprinkled my experience with bitterness. Still, there are veins and arteries of Amerika that make living here, tolerable. Despite my new found minority status, I find myself asking telemarketers where they are located whenever I detect a thick accent as they read a prepared pitch. Naturally, I cringe at the thought of outsourcing. It is no secret that Amerika is suffering, but amerikans continue to do well. All others find life challenging, normal.

Currently, Amerikans are pretending to have hope as they lose their jobs and give up their homes. Some are suicidal. Some are typical as they prey on the poor and gullible. Fortunately, others find greed amongst the fortunate.

And though, some Amerikans are homeless and jobless others continue to concern themselves with aesthetic issues like weight loss, tattoos, piercings, cosmetic surgery, immortality and eternal youth. Who will they impress if Amerika can't help those who have helped her?

We must save our sons. It is our duty to save our children. We must educate them without upholding and duplicating the methods of our oppressors and weakening the will of our young warriors. And if they are to be subjected to the penal system, we must be prepared to extract them legally or pack our bags to travel the journey that enables us to identify and extract the potential warrior or chance losing our sons and brothers to a system of corruption, sexual misbehavior, illiteracy, racism and denial of self or legacy.

Somethin' 'bout baz!

I do not have all the answers. Nor am I a psychiatrist, medical doctor, politician, liar or lawyer. However, I am serious about the upliftment and celebration of my people. I may be a social scientist of some sort. I am definitely a product of the *Black Power Movement*. Sure, I hold degrees from a eurocentric institution, but I am more proud of the contributions made by way of my Ancestors and the lessons provided by my elders. More importantly, the love I house for my people keeps me from bending to allow anyone to ride my back or shuffling to convenience others. At times, I may seem selfish or anti-*anything not black*, but I am not addicted to color because I have learned that color has yet to conquer the conditioning granted by the minds of greedy, self-serving, oppressive entities. And "colored" people condone anything issued or sanctioned from the thieving minds of their conniving oppressors.

The concealment of that which is obvious was never easy for me. And I haven't always been so damn reserved. Prison and the need to be calculating, analytical and undoubtedly "invisible" taught me to wear masks. Well, it was necessary at the time, but as a people we are running out of time. Be it me, any of the ethno-conscious forerunners, a YouTube sensation, a street lit author or some concerned mother – it is important that we increase the intensity of living as our Ancestors envisioned and the Creative Forces would have us live as a people.

I have given you a part of me. It is not fictitious. I wish that I could have embellished some parts of this book to make for a better read, but *it is what it is* and we need some doses of reality and bitterness to taint the acidic sweetness that we habitually lust for. I look forward to the day when a child grows to question me about my use of words, sexual *under*-tone, harsh criticisms and love for blackness.

For now - I am *baz moreno*. My Ancestors continue to speak. My pen continues to move. Thanks for sharing a page in my life.

Baz Moreno & Associates, LLC Order Form

Please Send:

_____copies of *Exodus from Enlightenment: Recognition of Blackness & War* ($20.95 ea.)

_____copies of *Extracting the Warrior: An Anthology of Prison Letters* ($8.99 ea.)

Shipping/Handling ($6 for 1 book and $4 for each additional book)
$_____

$_____ -

Send a form with check or money order made payable to:

Baz Moreno & Associates, LLC

903B Honey Creek Rd, #296

Conyers, GA 30013-3042

(404) 300-3945

Or send payment via *PayPal* to bazmoreno@gmail.com *or* call and request an invoice. You may order books at (online store) http://shop.bazmoreno.net/

Visit www.bazmoreno.net

Read baz's views -
http://unbiasedblackness.blogspot.com/